"Here's a book that breaks down the mechanics of skiing into simple terms. In my many years of racing and coaching I have heard methodologies, philosophies and theories of all sorts, but Ken's way of sharing his tips, insights and analogies is like sitting on the chair with him between runs, chatting skiing. He captures the essence and thrill of fluid, fast, fun skiing – but without the downhill suit – in a simple and informative way for easy understanding by skiers at all skill levels."

Rob Boyd ChPC
Sport Development Manager, Whistler Mountain Ski Club
Speed Coach, Canadian Alpine Ski Team
World Cup Downhill winner

"If you're looking for a simpler way to ski, read this book! If you think you know everything about skiing, read this book. This book takes you through Ken's straightforward approach towards skiing in all conditions and all turn shapes. His approach is not designed for the elite world cup athlete who is in top physical condition and skiing on the latest racing skis. His approach is designed for the common skier who wants to go out and experience the joy and freedom of skiing. The simple fact is that the more you know about skiing the more this book will melt your mind as you think through Ken's well thought out approach to skiing.

The mountain can be your own playground with an endless possibility of thrills and experiences. This book will help you get there!!"

Willy Raine
Canadian Olympic Ski Cross Gold Medalist Coach
Canadian Olympic Alpine Skier

"Ken's thorough insight into how he skis and what he feels is very informative and enlightening. Several times, I found myself nodding in agreement with Ken's thoughts and philosophy towards skiing. There are so many great ideas and hints in this book and I'm sure I will refer to it often. I specifically enjoyed the "What to try" sections. The use of diagrams and illustrations also help the reader to further understand Ken's comments and ideas. I feel that skiers of all abilities will benefit from reading Ken's book."

Tomio Fukumura
Alpine Race Coach
Head Coach Masters Program, Whistler Mountain Ski Club
Former Japanese National Team Coach - Men's World Cup SL Team

How I Ski

"Ken Chaddock is one of the rare skiers who can relate the act of skiing to engineering and physics and translate it to understandable thoughts. An accomplished skier himself it upholds his teachings that he started skiing as an adult and has used his own tactics to learn the art far greater than most. I applaud the skier and his book."

Chris Kent
Canada Alpine Ski Team 1979-1986
Lifelong skier

"Ken's account of how he skis is thorough, exact and well depicted. He shares many insights, techniques and tips for the curious skier who is eager to improve."

Mark Anderson
Racing coach, Whistler Mountain Ski Club & Dave Murray Ski Camps
Canadian Alpine Ski Team Alumnus

"I enjoyed reading Ken's book. I found it easy to read and understand; it contains many unique ideas expressed with carefully chosen words that describe skiing in ways that I haven't found in other ski books.

I recommend it for anyone interested in skiing…and learning English!"

Akiko Takemoto
CSIA Level 4 Ski Instructor, SIA
Japan, Whistler Blackcomb

"A typical skier standing at the top of a hill doesn't think about how they will adapt their technique for the upcoming slope and conditions. They simply know how to get down the hill using turns or a reasonable facsimile, and off they go, repeating moves learned through trial and error or as taught to them by their family, friends or ski instructor of long ago. This works. But it can be hard work and not very pretty.

For some this is not enough!

Ken's insightful analysis allows a dedicated intermediate or expert skier to launch themselves to the next level and beyond. Understanding precisely what to do and why will allow you to improve your skiing—more control with less effort—and you will even look better!"

Steve Podborski
Olympic Medalist and World Cup Overall Downhill Champion
Canadian Alpine Ski Team

ISBN   1481112961
EAN-13 9781481112963

Fourth edition. Incorporates refinements based on new insights gained through applying the content of earlier editions when skiing and teaching.

NOTE FROM THE AUTHOR: Skiing and teaching ski technique is a lifelong journey for me, and my approach continues to evolve. For further insights please feel free to browse www.skiwellsimply.com. Thanks!

Synopsis

Mastering alpine skiing can be a long and bewildering pursuit given all the factors to be discovered and tamed. This book dissects expert skiing into a handful of movements and focuses that when integrated produce fearless and exciting skiing. It uses a first person perspective and clear explanations for easy comprehension by novice and advanced skiers alike. It describes key body movements for expert skiing, how to do them, what they feel like, when to apply them, and how to practice them both on and off the hill *(before your next ski trip)*. It also includes tips for different terrain and snow conditions. Its goal is to help you improve your knowledge and skill so you can enjoy skiing to its utmost.

Foreword

I've often pondered: "what is the ultimate point of excellent skiing technique?" In ski racing, excellent technique makes it possible to be competitive; the 'point' being to ski fast—consistently fast—through race courses. In recreational skiing, the 'point' varies from person to person. Some seek simply to ski without fear. Others seek to impress with finesse. Many find the pursuit of learning to be highly motivating, and the resulting increase in skill highly satisfying. Personally, I'm constantly searching for new knowledge and understanding—so I can continue to ski better, with more ease and more fun, on any slope and on any type of snow. On a hard snow day, I like to park arcs on groomed runs. On a powder day, I savor the steep and deep. Whatever the conditions, I relish how the snow comes 'alive' under my feet as I zip from turn to turn.

I discussed "what's the ultimate point" with a long time friend and former national ski team member who has taught skiing for over thirty years. He simplified it to "Ken, just teach them to ski like you do and they'll be more than happy." This book aims at the heart of his advice.

Ken Chaddock
Whistler, Canada

My primary career as a professional engineer immersed me in the development, marketing and sales of wireless data communications systems and related software solutions. During that time, I earned a reputation for distilling complex topics into a few key points that were pivotal to a given objective or customer's interests. Alpine skiing is a pursuit that I began as an adult, with most of my learning about technique occurring in recent years. The freshness of my learning and my ability to pinpoint the keys that really 'make the difference' allow me to describe my skiing, especially how and why it works, in concise and simple terms. My goal is to provide you with a clear understanding of my own 'distilled' approach to skiing in order to help you advance your understanding and enjoyment of this very alluring and captivating sport.

Table of Contents

How This Book Should Help You

The better I ski the more I enjoy skiing

For me, skiing offers many delights: the camaraderie of people having fun, the beauty of the mountain environment, the thrill of zipping over snowy terrain, the flow of my body through space and the forces I feel underfoot, and, the great memories I get to replay at après-ski.

I discovered long ago that how much I enjoyed a given day correlated strongly with how good every run felt, independent of snow conditions, terrain or weather. As my technique improved, each run felt better and each day brought more opportunities for great moments and memories. Better technique enabled me to have more fun with my skiing—and to ski more runs with more confidence and less effort. Technique became my key to enjoying skiing more, as in more days and more fun each day.

Skillful technique to me means applying skiing-specific movements timed to the forces I feel up through my feet so my skis carry me along a line of travel at a speed that I choose. My aim with this book is to help you improve your skiing quickly by distilling my knowledge from years of free skiing, racing and teaching into a handful of critical focuses that produce fun and exciting skiing. My approach is to share my skiing—what I do, what I focus on, and how it feels—to give you insights that you can explore in order to advance your skiing.

My skiing credentials include big mountain skiing, ski racing and ski instruction, with countless days observing and analyzing my and other people's skiing. I have skied at Whistler Blackcomb since 1972, averaging 50-60 days each year, and recently 125 and more days per season. I've been taught by the best in ski racing and ski instructing circles and often receive compliments about my skiing from top level coaches and seasoned skiing professionals—which convinced me that I have something worth sharing, hence this book.

How I Ski

On the teaching side I've helped skiers at all skill levels, experts through intermediates through 'never-evers' (some who have never seen snow before). I use the principles in this book with all skill levels, selecting focuses according to the skill level at hand. Even early stage skiers grasp the basics of balance and key body movements, given clear and simple explanations. Intermediate and advanced skiers are usually quick to 'get' the key movements and apply them to improve their skiing. Expert skiers gain from the 'inside' view, comparing and reflecting relative to their own understanding to develop a more complete view of skiing. Feedback has been rewarding. "This is the best lesson I've had in years...and I've had a lot of lessons", "I've never gotten my skiing to feel so good before", and (my favorite) "I never knew it could be this easy". The success I've enjoyed with helping aspiring skiers makes me confident that if you read, understand and work with the principles in this book, you *will* improve your skiing.

My goal is to provide you with a clear and concise formula for expert skiing that you can read within a short time, and carry with you for quick review. Early pages summarize my skiing model. I then detail the specific techniques I use—there is only a handful—within that model. I follow with key postures and movements, and how you can practice each without needing to be on skis and out in the cold—virtually anywhere will do—at an airport, in the kitchen, or in front of the TV. I round out the book with tips for different skiing situations, i.e., groomed runs, moguls, trees, powder, steeps, a recap and review of selected points, and a section on troubleshooting typical foibles. The book concludes with nuggets of wisdom gleaned through decades of experience. Throughout, I've incorporated easy-to-spot *Tip, Insight,* and **What to try** boxes to help you 'get' what I'm describing.

Here's wishing you an enjoyable read, and many great skiing moments and memories to come.

To do something well is to enjoy it

1 The Basics

Small tilt

ski tracks its
sidecut

Big tilt

ski tracks its
lengthwise bend

Figure 1. When our skis slide lengthwise, the sharpness of our turns is determined by the tilt we give our skis and the pressure that our speed-affected weight generates downwards through their waists. At low tilts and speeds, the curve that our skis carry us along closely matches their sidecut. At higher tilts and speeds, the curve they travel closely matches their lengthwise bend.

How I Ski

Skis and why they turn themselves

A ski has curved sides or edges, or a 'sidecut', its waist being narrower than its tip and tail. Most modern skis also have an upwards bend, or 'rocker', near their tip and possibly tail. When we tilt a ski slightly and balance on it, its edge contacts the snow mainly along the curve of its sidecut. If we then allow the ski to slide forward slowly along its edge, it will seek to carry us along this same line of contact and deliver a gentle shallow turn. As we tilt the ski more and allow our speed to increase, its sidecut and rocker shape in combination with our weight bends the ski along its length and sharpens the curve that the ski will seek to carry us along. Notably, at higher tilts and speeds the pressure on the ski can be several times our stationary body weight, which bends the ski even more than just tilting it and standing on it while stationary. Depending on how much it is tilted, pressured and bent, a ski can deliver a surprisingly sharp turn.

Figure 1 summarizes the effect of ski tilt on lengthwise bend and sharpness of turn.

When skiing we tilt our skis according to the turns we want them to carry us along. For our skis to turn reliably and predictably we need to stand 'centered' on them. Ski boots help us do just that.

Ski boots and what 'centered' means

Ski boots encase our lower extremities and clamp them to long 'turning tools' called skis. Our boots allow us to tilt our skis side to side so they turn and carry us along a desired line of travel. Our boots also help us stand 'centered and balanced' so our skis turn readily and easily.

We are centered whenever we feel equal pressure on our shins and calves from the cuffs of our ski boots and equal weight on the balls and heels of our feet. *When we stand centered, the midpoint of where we feel our weight on the soles of our feet is our 'centerpoint'.* Figure 2 illustrates 'centered'.

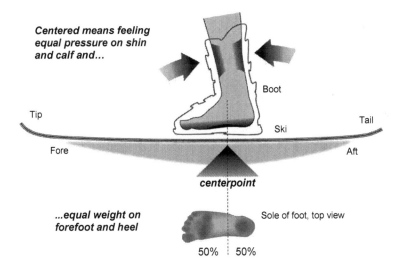

Figure 2. How our ski boots feel against our feet and lower legs when we stand stationary with weight centered in the fore and aft direction. When skiing, the distribution of weight that we feel on the soles of our feet reflects the distribution of pressure that our skis impart to the snow.

My preferred centerpoint is where my arch meets my heel, directly under my tibia, the major weight bearing bone of my lower leg. Your preferred centerpoint may be a little different, as long as it is a point where you can keep your weight centered while carrying a sizeable weight in addition to your own. Imagine carrying a friend piggyback-style while you ski along—where would you want your weight to be centered?

When our weight acts through our centerpoint and the waists of our skis, our skis perform reliable and predictable turns. Balancing so our weight acts through the waists of our skis contributes to our skiing fun and enjoyment. Balanced as such our skis feel more stable and predictable from turn to turn—which boosts our confidence and allows us to ski with more courage and panache.

How I Ski

During a turn, we balance mostly on our 'outside' ski, which is the ski that travels the outer perimeter of a turn (and beside the 'inside' ski). We should feel equal pressure from our boot on the shin and calf of our outside leg, significant pressure along the arch side of our outside boot (to hold our ski tilted on the snow), with most of our weight distributed along the ball, arch and heel of our outside foot.[1]

Ski poles and what they are for

Poles are useful for pushing around on flat areas and for leaning on in lift lines in order to look cool...   Mainly though, *poles are for helping to balance, especially while in motion*.

I use my poles to sense two things, the orientation of my body relative to the slope of the hill, and the texture and firmness of the snow. Both are important inputs for predicting how my skis will respond during upcoming turns. During a turn I *lightly* drag the tip of my inside pole along the snow. Just after the turn ends, I touch or plant my outside pole to preserve or improve my balance as I flow to the next turn. What I feel up through my hands and arms adds to what I feel from my boots and see with my eyes. My poles thus help gather valuable input for my brain and central nervous system to use in guiding my movements and reactions.

As a bonus, dragging my pole tip encourages me to keep my arms and upper body quiet. A quiet and steady upper body gives my eyes a smooth ride so I see a stable view of the upcoming terrain. The better I'm able to see, the better I'm able to predict how the upcoming snow will feel up through my skis and feet, and the more likely I am to achieve what I intend to.

---

[1] When I am balanced, I feel my weight distributed along the whole of my feet, toes through heels. This gives me maximum stability and helps me stay balanced amidst the jostling and turbulence that I encounter while skiing. The ability to ski while being aware of how our boots feel against our lower legs and the bottoms of our feet is *'to ski with sole'*... (That's my first pun!)

My skiing is centered on balance *(pun intended!)*

My goal is to have my skis perform the turns I intend while gravity powers me down a mountainside. ***Turns are my means to freedom, fun and safety.*** To have my skis make turns for me I tilt them and balance on them while progressively adjusting how I am standing, my movements and muscular efforts timed to the changes in weight I predict and then feel on the soles of my feet.

My skiing consists of tilting my skis, predicting how my skis will turn, and balancing in postures that are strong enough to withstand the weight I feel while they turn.

Whether sliding quietly along a gentle slope, arcing high speed turns, or bounding down a field of moguls, balance is fundamental to skiing. It also carries an inherent plus: *if I'm balanced, I'm not falling!*

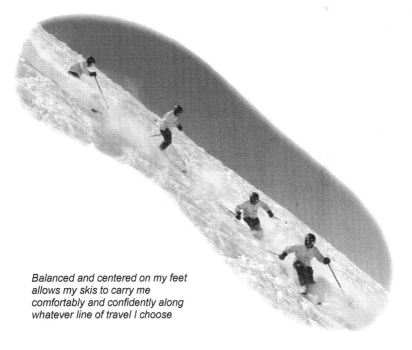

Balanced and centered on my feet allows my skis to carry me comfortably and confidently along whatever line of travel I choose

2 My Skiing Model

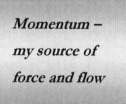

Momentum – my source of force and flow

My lazy self wants my skis to carry me where I choose for a minimum of effort. I use momentum to help my skis perform a turn, and then propel me smoothly into the next turn. Using momentum allows me to ski in a continuum of turn, transition, turn, transition, playing with the terrain and enjoying each run to its utmost.

What is momentum and where does it come from? Physics tells us that momentum is mass times speed, or more accurately, mass times velocity, velocity being speed in a given direction. *Whenever I am in motion—sliding along on skis—I have momentum.* Simply put, more speed means more momentum.

Converting momentum into pressure on my skis and exploiting that pressure is core to my skiing. When I tilt my skis, and stay centered and balanced, my weight presses through their waists and bends them lengthwise. The tilt and lengthwise bend of my skis curves my line of travel into a 'turn'.

The beauty of using momentum is that I can have my skis carry me where I want to travel by doing something that is familiar—standing and balancing. I don't have to 'turn' my skis, I just have to adjust them and balance on them. *When I tilt my skis and balance on them (skillfully), my skis turn me, rather than me turning them!*

> ### "It is our job to balance…and it's our skis' job to turn"
>
> My skiing is about tilting my skis, or 'turning tools', and balancing on them so they carry me along a desired line of travel at a desired speed. As swinging is to a hammer, tilting and balancing is to a ski…

> **INSIGHT** At higher speeds, the weight I feel in each turn can be significant, two to three times my static weight and more (my static weight is what appears on my bathroom scale). In a turn, more weight means more edge pressure, more lengthwise bend, and a more positive feel from the skis while they turn. Often, the apex of the turn feels *as stable as standing on a rock ledge.* The confidence such stability brings, plus feeling my weight vary dramatically between light and heavy, makes for fun and exciting skiing.

Balancing the barbell

Since momentum is central to my skiing and mass is tightly related to momentum, I find it helpful to picture what the mass distribution is of my body plus equipment and clothing. The upper-to-lower mass distribution of the human body by itself is about 60:40. With boots, skis, poles, clothing, helmet, etc. factored in, as when skiing, it approaches 50:50. Hence, I envision my mass while skiing to resemble a barbell that is balanced on end, its upper weight, the center of mass of everything above my hip joints (hips, torso, head, arms and poles) balanced over its lower weight, the center of mass of everything below my hip joints (legs, feet, boots and skis). I 'hold' the lower weight of the barbell at my centerpoint, and move my centerpoint around in order to balance the barbell. Figure 3 depicts how the imaginary barbell relates to a skier; the upper weight lodged in the skier's chest and the lower weight between their shins.

To be balanced, the barbell must be in line with the vector sum of all forces acting on it. When standing still the only force is gravity, pulling downwards in a purely vertical direction. Any deviation of the barbell from pure vertical introduces a sideways-acting 'tipping force' on the upper weight of the barbell that acts to make it (and me) fall over.

Figure 3. View of skier (yours truly!) showing imaginary barbell that represents the mass distribution of body plus equipment.

When skiing, sideways-acting 'deflection forces' accompany any change to my line of travel. Deflection forces feel like extra weight on my feet during each turn and 'deflect' my total mass left or right from the line that it would otherwise travel due to momentum and gravity alone.

To be balanced at mid turn the barbell must be oriented so that net tipping forces are zero. The greater the deflection forces, the heavier I feel, and the more noticeably any out-of-balance imperfections convert into tipping forces. My posture must also be strong enough to withstand the heaviest weight I feel (and am!) at the apex of each turn, where my line of travel is changing most quickly. *When I am balanced in a turn I have no sensation of tipping forces; I only feel heavier, more so the higher the speed or the tighter the turn.*

Between turns, the lower weight of the barbell needs to cross under its upper weight so it is reoriented to balance atop the combination of gravity plus deflection forces that arise in the new turn. Figure 4 summarizes these points.

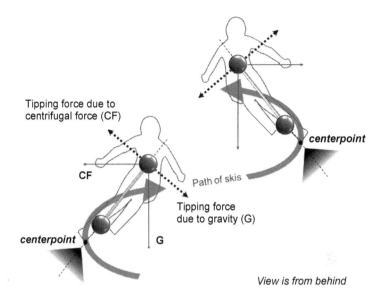

Figure 4. For perfect balance during each turn, the tipping forces on the upper weight of the barbell due to centrifugal force (CF) and gravity (G) must cancel each other exactly. Between turns, the barbell must be reoriented so tipping forces will again cancel in the next turn.

Moving the lower weight around is the only real means I have to balance my internal barbell. There's no big hand or sky hook available to shift my upper mass sideways, or save it from a fall. *In order to balance I adjust my skis so they move my feet around under my upper body, striving to have my weight always feel centered on my feet.*

A clarification:

I use the barbell analogy to help describe how my skiing works and feels rather than to precisely describe the physics of skiing. A barbell-like mass distribution reflects that my legs plus skis and boots have significant weight, and that balance requires the pressure I feel pushing up through the soles of my feet to be in line with the forces I feel weighing me down.

How I Ski

The barbell describes only the orientation of the upper and lower centers of mass, rather than the specific position of body parts or limbs. For instance, Figure 3 shows the torso is quite vertical relative to the tilt of the barbell. Likewise, the tilt of the skis is only roughly perpendicular to the barbell; 'edging' further sets the tilt at which the skis engage the snow.

Achieving rhythm and flow

I ski by linking "turn, transition, turn, transition..." During a turn, I balance centered on tilted skis. Between turns, I flow into a posture that is aligned to balance atop the forces I predict in the upcoming turn. During each turn, I feel heavier than normal while gravity plus deflection forces act on me. During each transition, I feel light in weight while momentum carries me towards the next turn.

During each turn I balance mostly on my outside foot with just a little weight on my inside foot for added stability. I focus on balance which helps keep my upper body quiet, just 'along for the ride'. I hold my arms extended and out to the front and side as a tightrope walker would, and let my inside pole tip drag lightly on the snow to help me sense how my body is oriented relative to the slope. When my skis have turned enough so they will carry me towards where I want my next turn to begin, I stop resisting the forces of the turn and let momentum take over.

During the transition, I let momentum take my feet across under my torso and my torso across over my feet. ***This momentum-driven lateral transposition of my feet and torso, or 'switch', helps me flow smoothly from one turn to the next with little physical effort.*** Figure 5 shows how the simultaneous crossunder and crossover creates an "X" from the exit of one turn to the entry of the next.

My 'X-Factor'

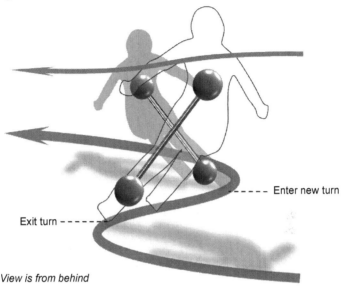

Exit turn - - - - -

Enter new turn - - - - -

View is from behind

Figure 5. During each transition, the relative positions of my feet and upper body at the exit of one turn and the start of the next create an "X" when viewed along my momentum-driven line of travel.

INSIGHT *Using momentum to reorient my body between turns is my skiing 'X-Factor'.*

Until I paid specific attention to using the flow of my skis to drive my switch, I never realized how effectively this rarely-talked-about 'move' simplifies skiing. It takes little physical effort, but does require predicting accurately where my skis will take my feet, and timing precisely when to let momentum take over.

To trigger my switch I simply let momentum take over—letting my torso go with its momentum and my feet and skis go with theirs. I briefly maintain the tilt on my skis so they will carry my feet across under me while my torso and viewpoint (eyes) glide across and over my feet toward the inside of the upcoming turn. My goal is to have momentum reorient my mass so I am balanced going into the next turn.

It often feels (especially at speed) as though the snow rises and falls under me as I flow out of one turn and into the next. Sometimes there is indeed a real rise in the snow, especially in moguls, but mostly the hump is 'virtual'; I feel it even though there is no real rise in the snow. This 'virtual hump' occurs early in my switch, and lofts my mass upwards to the extent that I absorb, resist, or assist its effect. When I time my effort and movement well to its upward boost, I feel light in weight until I arrive where I've planned my next turn to begin. Figure 6 depicts using the hump to get light in weight, then extending (getting taller) while preparing to 'land' where my weight increases going into the next turn. Besides the fun of feeling light, being light gives me the freedom to adjust my balance and posture for the next turn with very little effort.[2]

> **INSIGHT   The Virtual Hump effect**   As I exit a turn momentum moves my body mass (internal barbell) from the tilted orientation it was balanced in during the turn towards a vertical orientation that it passes through at mid-transition en route to the next turn. Also late in the turn, my feet and skis progress from traveling down the slope to somewhat across it, which levels their line of travel (more so with tighter turns on steeper slopes). In combination, *these factors create a "virtual hump"—it feels like the snow rises then falls as I flow through the transition.*

---

[2] On a smooth groomed slope I can become completely weightless (airborne) between turns by seeking heavy weight in the turn followed by a quick switch in which I resist (or even assist) rather than absorb the virtual hump. In moguls it is very easy to become airborne since the hump is more real than apparent; here, I often need to absorb the bump (by actively retracting my legs) in order to keep my skis in contact with the snow.

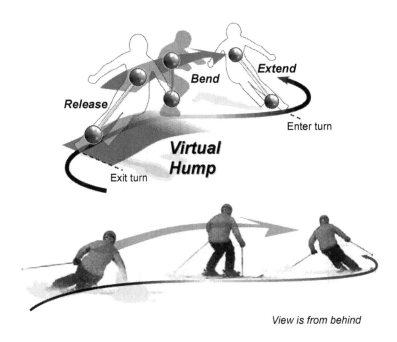

View is from behind

Figure 6. I use the virtual hump to get lofted and light – and add fun to my skiing. The underfoot pressure I feel early in my switch drives the loft and lightness I enjoy between turns. It's a mini terrain park, every turn.

Through the transition, I flex my legs shorter then longer while my feet cross under me. Doing so keeps my head traveling smoothly and my skis in contact with the snow. My head traveling smoothly provides a steady viewpoint from which to see and assess what I am approaching (and what is approaching me!) and my skis in contact with the snow allow me to adjust where my feet are under my torso so I can fine-tune my balance before my weight increases noticeably in the new turn.[3]

---

[3] 'Edging' my skis shifts my feet laterally as my skis respond to their tilt, pressure and lengthwise bend. 'Pivoting' my skis adds friction that shifts my feet along the direction that momentum is carrying me, that is, along my 'line of momentum'. Notably, the lighter I feel the less my skis are pressured on the snow and hence the less able they are to affect my direction and speed.

At mid transition, I pass through a posture in which my hips and knees are quite bent and my skis are flat on the snow. Thereafter, the distance from my upper body to the snow increases. Since I don't weigh very much during this time, I can extend with ease, 'lowering' my feet to keep my skis on the snow.

I practice 'patience' before the turn. As I extend and while I'm still light in weight, I allow my skis to find their preferred track or direction based on their tilt, pressure and lengthwise bend. I balance most of my weight, however little of it there is, on my new outside foot (and ski) with just enough weight on my inside foot to help me balance and stabilize rotationally. *Balancing on tilted skis* in a posture that is ready for a big increase in weight *before pressure builds in the new turn* confirms my patience.

Any loft I've enjoyed from the virtual hump eventually ends and I 'land' on the snow again, feeling my weight increase quickly. I smooth out the increase in weight to avoid landing with a 'bang', easing my skis onto and into the snow. This way, they pick up their turn predictably, reliably, and smoothly. As my weight increases, and as the turn begins, my focus becomes balancing atop the forces I feel pushing up through my feet and judging when to exit the turn.[4]

Figures 7 and 8 illustrate my overall flow as I ski turn to turn. Figure 7 shows the orientation of my internal barbell in relation to my line of travel. Figure 8 captures where I feel heavy then light then heavy from one turn to the next.

---

[4] Usually my weight is mostly on my outside foot during a turn. Sharing weight more equally on both feet is more likely to occur in deep powder and in moguls, for added stability and strength.

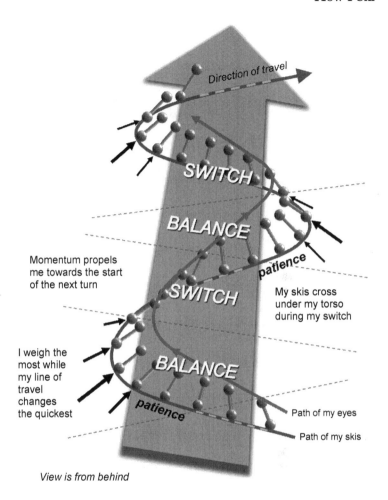

View is from behind

Figure 7. Barbell action while skiing turn to turn. Arrows indicate the direction and magnitude of upwards acting underfoot force that my internal barbell (body mass) is balanced over during each turn. Between turns, my skis carry my feet across under the momentum-driven trajectory of my upper body.

Figure 8. From one turn to the next my weight changes noticeably—heaviest during the turn, and lightest during the transition. *My lightness between turns gives me the freedom to edge and aim my skis with very little effort.* I then fine-tune my balance and posture during a patient instant before resisting the forces of the next turn. Note how the skis cross under the torso which travels near straight while I'm light (middle images).

Whenever I feel light, it means that my skis are pressured lightly on the snow and thus susceptible to skidding—sliding a little sideways of where they point instead of sliding purely lengthwise with tails tracking tips. Unless I want to reduce my speed, I try to minimize or prevent skidding since skidding makes my skis less likely to carve reliably or slide smoothly, especially on hard snow or ice. To encourage them to slide cleanly along their edges I consciously aim my skis along their line of travel while I edge them in preparation for the new turn. ***Edging and aiming my skis without injecting rotational influences from my upper body (which could pivot and skid my skis undesirably) is critical to my skiing.***[5]

---

[5] I describe in a later section how I move in order to 'edge' and 'aim' my skis.

When balanced in a turn I feel heavy, my upper and lower centers of mass aligned with the combined forces of gravity and deflection. Between turns, I feel light as momentum propels me, with just enough weight on my feet so my skis arc across under me for a good transposition of my feet and upper body. *Using momentum in this manner—balance and resist, release and flow—helps me ski a continuum of smoothly linked turns, each turn driven by deflection forces, and each transition driven by momentum.*

Seeing and judging what lies ahead

I look well ahead to plan where I want to travel. I make the ride for my eyes as smooth as possible, with a minimum of jostling and jarring about. I imagine my legs being a suspension system, which they are, and my arms a balancing pole such as a circus performer might use during a high wire act. This imagery helps me maintain a quiet flight path for my eyes, which improves my ability to assess the upcoming terrain.

I continually scan ahead to plan where my turns will begin, that is, where my skis will be when my weight escalates in each turn. During each transition I assess the snow where the immediate turn will begin, watching for surprises such as lumps of ice, sharp ripples, or rare but respect-demanding rocks. I adjust for any nuances then prepare my balance and posture before the weight increase of the new turn begins.

I enter each turn with an exit direction in mind—the direction along which momentum will propel me en route to the subsequent turn. Having an exit direction in mind as I enter a turn helps me exit the turn as intended, on plan and flowing into my transition.

Seeing and judging the upcoming snow and terrain helps me predict how my skis will react and what line of travel they will carry me along: a smooth view is a valuable input to smooth fun skiing. Figure 9 and the table that follows summarize my skiing model.

Feeling my weight alternating heavy and light, hearing the wind in my ears, and seeing the terrain zip by smoothly under me are things I cherish with every ski run …

Figure 9. My skiing model. Blending dynamic movements to tilt my skis and balance atop the resulting forces while enjoying the ride from turn to turn.

My skiing – summarized

Turn — Balance – Resist – Persist

- **Balance**: Prepare for the upcoming turn: flow into a 'ready-to-feel-heavy' posture with legs turned and weight centered mostly on the arch side of the outside foot.

- **Resist**: Hold against the weight of the turn, maintain posture, balance on a steady centerpoint, drag inside pole tip.

- **Persist**: Keep legs turned until momentum will take skis (and feet) towards where the next turn is to begin.

Transition — Release – Switch – Extend – Edge

- **Release**: Stop resisting the weight of the turn, let momentum take feet and upper body, retract legs as needed to keep skis on snow.

- **Switch**: Let feet cross under torso, turn legs to keep skis sliding with tails tracking tips while momentum carries the upper body towards the inside of the upcoming turn.

- **Extend**: Reduce bend in the knees and hip joints to keep skis on the snow while the distance increases between torso and snow.

- **Edge**: Turn legs to fine-tune tilt of the skis in preparation for the new turn (*turn thighs using legs only; no upper body movement*).[6]

---

[6] *Turning the legs ranks first in my skiing*, and is described in depth in the upcoming section.

3   Techniques in Motion

My skiing integrates a handful of techniques that are easier to realize while sliding along on a pair of skis than to mimic while standing still. This section describes each and its role in the turn-transition cycle. Look for *'What to try'* and *'Tip'* inserts for helpful drills and focuses to work with on hill in order to help you feel what I'm describing.

Legs turn, torso rides

Because the crux of my skiing is balance, and balance is achieved by having my feet well-placed relative to my upper body, and, since my feet and lower legs experience every force acting on me, my approach is to initiate any adjustments to the tilt and aim of my skis using only my legs.

My leading movement to control and adjust the tilt and aim of my skis is turning my legs, specifically my femurs, relative to my pelvis. Turning the legs without turning the pelvis allows me to adjust the tilt and aim of my skis while keeping my act of balancing simple. A steady pelvis means a steady upper body, and staying in balance is simpler with this approach than if I were to tilt or turn my upper body, or otherwise shift its mass around, in order to help tilt or aim my skis.

Note that any adjustment to my skis through turning the upper legs is only relative to the basic tilt and aim as driven by my posture and the orientation of my body to the slope. Turning the legs offers a quick and effective means to fine-tune the response of my skis with minimal disruption to my balance. Though how my skis respond and where they carry me is primarily due to the quality of my balance and my ability to deal with the forces of the turn, turning the upper legs is my key means to initiate, fine-tune and adjust from that baseline.

Figure 10 illustrates the leg moves I use to control the tilt and aim of my skis. *Turning my legs but not my feet controls the tilt* (or edge angle) of my skis, and *turning my legs and my feet controls the aim* (or direction) of my skis.

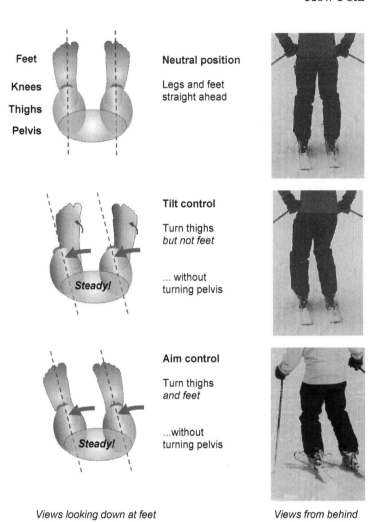

Feet

Knees

Thighs

Pelvis

Neutral position

Legs and feet
straight ahead

Tilt control

Turn thighs
but not feet

... without
turning pelvis

Steady!

Aim control

Turn thighs
and feet

...without
turning pelvis

Steady!

Views looking down at feet   *Views from behind*

Figure 10. Leg movements relative to the pelvis that control tilt and aim of
the skis. Movements shown are for turns to the left; mirror images would
show movements for turns to the right. Both legs turn in unison, equally yet
independently.

What to try

Tilt control   Stand on a flat area with your skis apart about the width of your hips. Without letting your pelvis or feet change direction, turn both upper legs in unison so both knees point right and left in unison. Notice the effect on the tilt of your skis. Repeat with your knees more bent. Note that more knee bend yields more change in ski tilt.

Aim control   Now lift one ski 3 or 4 inches. Turn your raised leg left and right so your knee, foot and ski all turn in unison (don't just turn your foot!). Notice that your ski aims wherever your knee points, regardless of how much your knee is bent.

*When doing either of the above, **be sure to keep your pelvis steady—neither rotating nor rocking side to side.** Those are strictly après-ski moves...*

INSIGHT   Because movements that affect my skis are so tightly coupled to balancing, I want to move in a way that readily adjusts the tilt and aim of my skis without complicating my ability to balance. Hence, *I isolate any effort related to tilting and aiming my skis to my legs only, with zero contribution from my upper body*.

I purposefully avoid tilting or turning my pelvis and hips, rotating my upper body, or bending sideways at my midsection, since doing any of these is likely to impart forces to my skis that I will then need to compensate for in my balancing act. Leaving my upper body decoupled from the turning of my legs minimizes the number of variables my central nervous system needs to deal with, so keeps my act of balancing as simple as possible.

Turning the legs <u>without involving the upper body</u> enables me to adjust my skis with precision, quickness and strength. Keeping rotational efforts or influences from the upper body at or near zero helps my skiing in several ways. I can adjust my skis with a minimal shift in where my body mass is relative to my feet—this keeps my act of balancing simple; I don't risk shifting body mass around and triggering reactions from my skis that may be difficult to counteract. I can impart tilt and aim to my skis with precision, 'dialing' the amount of adjustment by how much to the left or right relative to my pelvis that I turn my legs or point my knees. And, I can do so with strength, since the major muscles involved are in the upper leg and pelvic region. The upper legs as my 'engines of turn' allow me to fine-tune the tilt and aim of my skis, quickly and effectively, to suit what I need them to achieve.[7]

Moving only my legs to initiate edging and aiming of my skis affects in the simplest manner possible where my skis and feet move around under my torso. Keeping my upper body as a 'follower' prevents it from injecting impulses that cause my skis to skid or unnecessarily challenge my balance. My upper body never initiates: it is a willing and cooperative passenger. ***"Legs turn, torso rides" ranks foremost in my skiing.***

INSIGHT   To balance and ride, I want my skis to deliver a predictable line of travel based on their tilt, pressure and bend. Knowing where my skis and feet will soon be makes balancing that much easier. I avoid influences from my upper body that can interfere with what I anticipate my skis will do—thus my emphasis on turning the legs without involving the upper body. I also manage carefully the turning effort of my feet. Turning the legs makes it very easy to also turn or pivot the feet. Too much pivoting effort forces the skis into a skid. Sometimes I want a skid (to control my speed) but mostly I want to work with the direction that my skis choose. To do this I power tilt and aim adjustments to my skis by turning my thighs, then fine tune as necessary using the lesser strength of my ankles and feet. If no fine tuning is required, my ankles and feet remain quite relaxed, which enhances my ability to balance through terrain changes. My 'edging' action initiates from the upper legs, and moves down for fine-tuning. The often-referenced notion that edging the skis starts from the ground up—beginning with the ankles and feet to roll the skis onto edge—isn't part of my skiing.

---

[7] More tilt of the skis promotes tails tracking tips, less friction and more speed. Less tilt facilitates skidding of the skis, more friction and less speed. The ability to precisely 'dial' the amount of tilt and aim to our skis with a minimum of disruption to our balance adds significant versatility to our skiing.

What to try

To confirm isolation of ski tilt control from upper body (pelvis and
above) as well as your ability to balance while turning your legs, link
some turns on a groomed road or a very gentle run. Slide at
moderate speed standing centered in your boots—equal pressure
on shins and calves and equal weight on forefeet and heels. Now
point your knees left and right—turn *only* your thighs—so your skis
arc to the left and right accordingly. Relax your lower legs and
ankles to allow your skis to find their own track according to their tilt
and bend.

Leaving clean arcs and no signs of skidding between turns confirms
good isolation of movement between the upper body, legs, and feet.
Overtaking other skiers while turning continuously on a long gentle
road further confirms that you have your isolation working well.

As a further test, do the same while balancing on one ski at a time.
Clean arcs that show clearly where your ski tilted from one edge to
the other without any skidding confirms good isolation of leg turn
and foot direction—and great balance. Alternate every few turns
between turning moderately quickly (easiest) and s l o w l y (harder
to do). This drill develops balancing while turning the legs, and
offers effective use of time on less-than-challenging terrain.

Tip: drag both pole tips lightly on the snow to help succeed at these
drills. When progressing to one ski at a time, stand mainly on one
ski with it running flat and straight, and turn the other leg to edge the
lightly weighted ski side to side (just a little so you don't cross your
tips!). Once you see how your lightly weighted ski reacts to your leg
turns, slowly ease your weight onto it as you continue edging it side
to side. Be sure to isolate the turning of your leg from the direction
of your pelvis—aim for 100% isolation. [Hint: relax the pelvic region.]

Balance before the turn

To be in balance throughout a turn, I want to **be in balance before the turn begins.** When I enter a turn in balance, I am more likely to remain in balance throughout the whole turn. There are two requisites for being 'in balance': zero net tipping forces (see Figure 4 again), and a posture that is strong enough to withstand whatever weight I experience.

For zero tipping forces, I need to be exactly balanced with my weight acting through a steady centerpoint. I pay special attention to what my skis are doing, or what I'm doing to them, before the new turn begins in earnest. Why? During this time, my skis are lightly pressured and near flat on the snow—so are less certain to track reliably according to their tilt, pressure and bend. To ensure their tip to tail flow, I use 'legs only' to **progressively aim my skis along the line I intend them and thus my feet to travel into the turn.** Having a good sense of where my feet will be makes it easier to balance going into the turn. Figure 11 and 12 shows turning of the legs and feet during the transition, from a spectator view, and from a first person view, respectively.

Figure 11. Images from Figure 9 placed side by side, sequenced in time from right to left. Note the knees and skis turning relative to the upper body, especially in the first (rightmost) three images. My leg and feet turning is timed to have the skis flow through the transition, tails following tips, while the skis roll through edge-to-flat-to-edge.

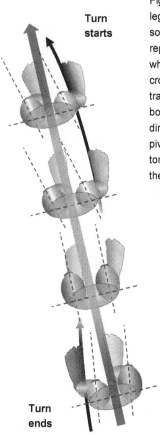

Turn starts

Turn ends

Figure 12. View looking down at pelvis, legs and feet during the transition. The soles of the feet are shaded to represent the relative weight I feel and where and when I feel it. Knees have crossed over the feet and skis by mid transition (second image from the bottom). Note that the skis change direction smoothly, there's no sudden pivoting. By the time the turn starts, my torso (pelvis and above) faces outside the direction of my feet and skis.

Through the transition I turn my legs and aim my feet to guide my skis predictably into the next turn

Torso follows momentum straight during the transition (wide arrow), while skis travel a curved line under me (narrow arrow)

Balancing throughout the turn also requires a posture that can resist the deflection-driven weight increase that I experience during the turn. If my posture isn't strong enough, I might collapse (fold completely at the hips or knees) or need to abandon the turn, neither of which is desirable. During the transition my goal is to arrive where the turn begins (where my weight increases) with my pelvis, chest and shoulders facing to the outside of the new turn, my outside leg extended enough (but less than fully straight!) to where it can withstand the upcoming weight of the turn, and my torso tilted a little forward at the hip joint. My goal is to flow into this ready-for-heavy-weight-with-skis-edged-for-grip posture with enough time for a patient instant before I feel my weight escalate in the new turn.

Balance on sufficiently edged skis

We've all experienced 'losing an edge' on a slippery patch of snow—as we enter a turn our skis suddenly slip sideways, leaving us falling to the inside of the turn. A first thought might be "my skis need sharpening" but the main causes of 'lose edge/fall inside' are insufficient tilt of the skis relative to the direction that our weight acts down through their edges, and, being out of balance—falling to the inside of the turn and hoping the anticipated edge grip of our skis will halt our fall. Figure 13 illustrates the difference between 'falling' and being 'balanced' early in the turn.

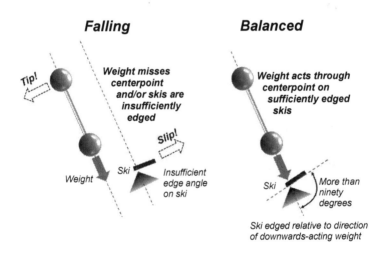

Figure 13a. Falling versus being balanced in a turn. Falling occurs when my weight and centerpoint are not in line with each other, worsened by a sideways slip if my skis are not tilted enough relative to the direction that my weight acts downwards through them.

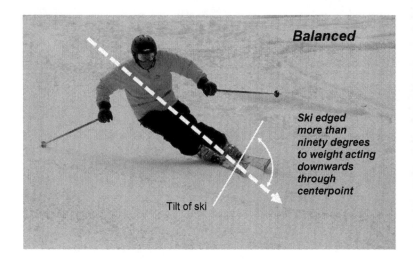

Balanced

Ski edged
more than
ninety degrees
to weight acting
downwards
through
centerpoint

Tilt of ski

Figure 13b. To ensure balance as my weight increases early in the turn, I want my weight acting exactly through my centerpoint, my skis edged so my weight pressing down through their edges encourages them to cut into the snow rather than slip sideways. This combination gives me something 'solid' to balance on during the turn.

INSIGHT   The posture best able to withstand heavy weight while holding our skis on edge varies from person to person. For me here's what works best: thighs turned at an angle to the pelvis, knees pointed inside of where the skis (and feet) point, torso tilted forward by bending at the hip joints (not the waist!), shoulders aligned with the pelvis (no twist in the spine), all balanced on a relatively long outside leg. This combo produces sufficient tilt on my skis that they don't slip out sideways, and a posture that can withstand a lot of weight.

Figure 14 shows entry to the turn from different viewpoints. Look for the relative direction of the chest, legs and skis as the skis begin to disrupt the snow (which marks where my weight increases and the turn begins).

Figure 14. Posture when entering the turn. My torso facing my line of momentum during the transition leads to it facing outside the direction of my skis as they enter the turn. Letting my upper body ride quietly while my skis respond to the turning of my legs sets up a strong, centered and relaxed posture going into the turn.

> **INSIGHT**   I do not actively turn my upper body to face to the outside of a turn. My upper body simply stays facing in line with momentum, which, as the turn progresses, increasingly points outside the turn. In essence, momentum pulls me in the direction I would travel if my skis suddenly lost their edge grip (more on this point later). While the skis change direction during the turn, I turn my legs and feet to match their changing direction; the result is a posture that can both carry a lot of weight *and* hold my skis tilted for a solid grip on the snow.

Balancing before the turn begins gives me an instant to get 'in sync' with the line that my skis will carry me along during the turn. I use this instant to fine-tune adjustments to posture and skis as required so I am fully ready for the upcoming turn. When I enter the turn in balance and anticipating the upcoming change in line and direction it will produce, tipping forces remain insignificant throughout the turn and I exit the turn as I entered it, in balance and facing where the new turn will begin. ***Balance before the turn is a key principle in my skiing.***

What to try

Stand on a reasonably steep hill with your skis facing across the slope, your knees slightly bent, and your pole tips on the snow to steady yourself. Balance with equal weight on both feet and equal pressure from your boot cuffs on your shins and calves. Without any other movement, turn both legs so your knees point a few degrees uphill of where your skis point.

Now, without changing where your knees point, face your pelvis (and torso, arms and head) a few degrees downhill of where your skis point, that is, knees towards eleven o'clock, pelvis towards one o'clock (or vice versa). Now, tilt your upper body forward by bending *straight forward at the hip joints* (leaning your upper body sideways is unnecessary). You should feel your weight move onto your downhill boot, seemingly automatically. Keep your legs turned so your weight concentrates along the arch side of your downhill boot.

What you feel when skiing through a turn should be similar, though more intense, since deflection forces *plus* gravity will be present.

Advance feet in the turn

During the turn, I want to continue the balance that I established before the turn. When I stay in balance, my skis perform predictable turns—and (so the saying goes) one good turn leads to another... The key 'sensor' that signals my quality of balance is how my boots feel against my lower legs and feet.[8]

My goal is to feel equal pressure on my shins and calves and a steady weight distribution along the arch and sole of my outside foot throughout the turn. To achieve this I advance my feet—mostly my outside foot—as the turn progresses. Figure 15 depicts the weight distribution I feel on the soles of my feet during the turn.

End of turn

I advance my outside foot in order to stay centered and balanced throughout the turn

Figure 15. Relative position of my feet during a turn. My goal is to keep the fore-aft weight distribution on the soles of my feet steady throughout the turn.

Shading indicates the relative weight or pressure I feel on the soles of my feet, darker signifying more pressure.

Start of turn

---

[8] I pay attention to such balance 'sensors' during my first run of the day, and infrequently after that. Too much thinking can really interfere with good skiing!

How I Ski

To move my feet forward I bend forward at the hip joints. A natural progression to the posture I move through at the entry to the turn, this move keeps me balanced on my outside foot. My extra weight during the turn acts to push my torso forward and, since my torso faces outside the line of the turn, 'over' my outside foot. Bending at the hip joints also lowers my overall body mass which increases my stability. It also positions my feet where they can rise in front of me in case I need to ski over a big rise in the snow—something that occurs often in large moguls.

While my focus is on advancing my outside foot, my inside foot also advances a little, especially in powder or moguls where my weight is closer to being equal on both feet. How far to move the feet? It seems counterintuitive for the feet to move ahead without having the weight shift back—and into the dreaded 'back seat'. The key is, ***don't move the feet too far!*** Simply seek equal pressure on your calves than shins.

Usually the distance my feet advance is about an ankle's width, though the goal is really to feel steady sensations from my boots, right from the beginning through the very end of the turn. Too little advance and my boot cuffs bang my shins, too much and my boot cuffs squash my calves. Just the right amount provides a solid and secure balanced feeling throughout the turn.[9]

My approach is to draw my feet back slightly during the transition to where they feel right 'under' me, then to ease them forward in order to keep the ***fore aft weight distribution on the soles of my feet constant***. I keep my upper body quiet and just along for the ride, unless I need to flex my whole body in order to deal with a big terrain change, or to make a big balance recovery (…sure glad that never happens…!). See Figure 16.

---

[9] I've been instructed to feel my weight mostly towards the ball of the foot early in the turn and mostly towards the heel late in the turn. While it is possible to ski like this, I find this weight shift unnecessary and risky, especially when I weigh a lot during turns. I seek steady fore and aft pressure on the soles of my feet, so any changes in fore and aft pressure serve as an early warning signal for 'going-out-of-balance'.

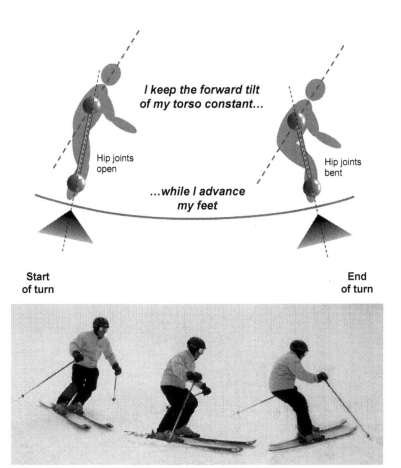

Start of turn

End of turn

Figure 16. The feet advance relative to the upper body during a turn in order to keep weight centered in the fore and aft direction throughout the turn. Hinging forward at the hip joints eases my feet forward, and, with my upper body facing a little to the outside of the turn, brings most of my weight onto my outside foot and ski.

Point knees inside

With the objective of perfect balance, besides advancing the feet, I also persist my leg-turning effort throughout the turn. This ensures that my skis keep doing their job, turning, while I do mine, balancing (and looking ahead) while my skis carry me through the turn.[10]

To help me point my knees sufficiently I imagine laser beams shooting out of my kneecaps and searing lines in the snow just inside the curve that my skis will soon trace. Figure 17 shows my leg-turning effort persisted right through the exit of the turn in order that my skis carry my feet across and under my upper body during the transition.

Mid to late in the turn

Figure 17. During the turn, I persist my leg turning effort to ensure my skis grip firmly at the heaviest part of the turn (it often feels as solid as a rock ledge!). At the exit of the turn, which is just beginning in the last image, I persist my leg turn so momentum will carry my feet across and under my upper body, and thus drive my switch.

---

[10] I'm a leg-turning balancer.

Advancing my feet keeps my weight centered fore and aft throughout the turn which helps my skis track reliably. Pointing my knees to the inside of the line that I want my skis to achieve ensures a strong grip of my skis on the snow and leads to having my skis carry my feet across under my upper body during the transition. The result is feeling perfectly balanced as I flow out of each turn. *'Advance feet in the turn' and 'point knees inside' the turn are important elements of my skiing technique.*

INSIGHT   You may have been told at some time to bend sideways at your waist or midriff in order to ensure weight or more edge angle on your outside ski. While getting weight on an edged outside ski is a good objective, bending sideways at the waist like a parenthesis mark to achieve it can be uncomfortable physically (ouch this hurts!) and emotionally (do I look as bad as I feel?). Worse, proactively tipping your upper body to the side complicates your efforts to balance (not helpful when balance is what we're striving for…!).

As I enter a turn on edged skis, they begin to turn and move my feet sideways under me. At the same time my momentum gently urges my upper body forward towards the perimeter, or outside, of the turn. When I hinge forward at the hip joints under this gentle urging from behind, doing so coaxes my outside foot forward and balances my upper body over my outside foot and ski. No conscious moving of the torso for me—no turning, twisting or tipping—rather, just a little forward bend at the hip joints in time with the forces I feel working on me (Simple!!).

[Note: Greater weight during aggressive turns facilitates balancing with a sideways bend in the hip joint in addition to a forward bend (more on this aspect in the next chapter).]

What to try

Maintaining perfect balance throughout the turn while moving your feet forward can be elusive. Find a gentle groomed slope where you can ski a series of turns *slowly*. Begin each turn by letting your internal barbell incline to become perpendicular to the slope so your skis briefly flatten on the snow. Your skis should start turning down the hill—seemingly automatically—without any other effort on your part.

As your skis start their turn, turn your legs and feet just enough to accommodate their change in direction. Turning your legs tilts the skis a little and leads to them completing the turn—provided you stay balanced. Hinging your torso forward at your hip joints as the turn progresses helps to balance your weight through your outside foot. The goal is to *keep unchanging and steady the fore aft distribution of weight on the soles of your feet, particularly the sole of your outside foot*. Throughout the turn, you should feel pressure along the arch side of the outside foot with weight on both the ball and heel of your foot.

Once you can replicate these moves and feelings at low speed, let your skis run faster so they carve or arc, and look for the same feedback from your boots, seeking a stable, balanced feeling throughout each turn. Your turns should seem automatic and happen reliably without requiring any mid-turn moves to correct your balance.

TIP   *"Skiing is a slice..."*

Imagine slicing the snow with the forward movement of your outside foot, using the edge of your outside ski like a giant knife to slice a giant tomato. This imagery can help you blend turning of the legs, balancing on the outside foot, and hinging at the hip joints into one smooth effort and movement. Salad, anyone?

Momentum drives the switch

The transition, with its switch and subsequent lightweight feeling, is a favorite for me because it feels like (and is...!) controlled flight, without quite being airborne.[11]

The transition begins when I let momentum 'take over'—I stop resisting the forces of the turn and let my upper and lower centers of mass follow their respective momentums to initiate my switch. ***My switch is more something that I let happen than make happen.***[12]

Figure 18. Images continued from Figure 17. I let momentum 'take over' to exit the turn. Momentum drives the switch—it's my X-Factor at play!

---

[11] Being airborne is OK too. A close friend coined the term "carving oxygen" after watching me launch from the uphill side of a mogul, fly the immediate trough, then carve down the backside of the subsequent mogul. It's still great fun!

[12] I've seen skiers trying to make their switch 'happen' by nodding their head forward (like a shadow head butt), or thrusting their hands and arms downhill, or attempting to shift their torso downhill by suddenly bending at the midsection. These moves are unnecessary and disruptive to balance and flow.

How I Ski

The 'Hump'

Early in the switch, I experience the 'virtual hump' as momentum carries my upper body across and over my feet. I exploit the hump in order to get light in weight and achieve 'float' during the transition. Depending on my speed and the terrain, I absorb (actively shorten by bending at the knees and hips), resist (hold everything as is), or pulse (actively extend) as my switch begins. ***My goal is to achieve lightness, yet 'fly' low enough so my skis remain in contact with the snow.***[13] Figure 19 depicts the upward thrust from the virtual hump.

Figure 19. As momentum reorients my body early in the transition, the virtual hump effect lofts my body away from the snow to the degree that I shorten, hold, or extend in height. Extending will usually pop me off the snow; lightness becomes weightlessness.

---

[13] To ski with élan [ey-*lahn*] is to ski with power and enthusiasm. I also aspire to ski with ballon [ba-*lawn*], an appearance of lightness and buoyancy. Skiing turns with élan leads to skiing transitions with ballon, assisted by the virtual hump.

Switch small to tall

At mid transition, I move through a flexed posture with my legs bent and my skis flat on the snow. From this 'small' posture, as in the foreground image in Figure 19, it's time to get 'tall', or extend, and prepare for the upcoming turn, as in the rightmost image in Figure 20.

As turn ends feel
the virtual hump

Extend from small
to tall while light

Balance and flow into
heavy-ready posture

get tall

be small

light in weight

Virtual hump

Figure 20. I move through 'small' early in the transition as I crest the virtual hump, then extend to 'tall' while I'm light in weight through the rest of the transition. While I'm light in weight, I flow into a 'heavy-ready' posture to prepare for the increase in weight that will accompany the upcoming turn. The lower diagram's double-headed arrows depict my extension, and its dark grey shading the relative weight I experience: first the boost from the virtual hump, then the subsequent float.

Through the rest of the transition, I focus on having my skis run cleanly while I tilt them to deliver the line I want to travel in the new turn. Until the turn begins, I enjoy a floating sensation and being able, with little effort because I'm light in weight, to extend and turn my legs in preparation for the upcoming turn. Importantly, *I extend, edge and aim using only my legs, without contributions from my torso or upper body*. Keeping my upper body simply following its momentum helps my skis arc cleanly even though they are lightly pressured. My goal is to avoid injecting any energy or influence from my upper body in order to keep my act of balancing simple and my skis aimed as desired while going into the turn. Figure 20 shows the relationship of the timing of the virtual hump and extension through the transition.

INSIGHT   To leave the security of a turn (and go where momentum may never have taken anyone before...) a feel good necessity is being confident about just where it is that momentum will be taking us! Thankfully, in the absence of deflecting forces (as in between turns) momentum carries us along a straight line—whatever direction we have when we stop resisting a turn will be our direction until the next turn begins.

After thousands of turns and transitions, I know what to expect when I let momentum take over at the end of a turn. While learning I would make my skis go flat in mid turn (to remove any deflecting forces) and see what direction I ended up traveling in.

My skiing is different than this learning move. Rather than let my whole mass (body plus boots and skis) travel the same line, I give my torso up to its momentum and my skis and feet up to theirs. With good centered balance late in the turn, I find it easy to predict the trajectories that my torso and skis will take. Momentum drives the switch.

What to try

Start a turn on a groomed slope, and then abandon it early before its normal 'end'. You'll find that your momentum determines your line of travel at the instant you exit the turn. Repeat several times, and then return to linking your turns, trying to predict the direction along which momentum will carry you between turns.

Turn knees (...then balance)

At or even before the middle of the transition, I turn my knees towards the inside of the new turn to encourage my skis to grip and begin the turn. I am careful to turn them only enough for that effect, since too much weakens my posture, and risks getting overly challenged by the weight of the next turn. Figure 21 shows images (left to right) beginning just after the virtual hump. In the first three images, I turn my thighs from where they suited the old turn to where they point my knees just inside the line of the new turn (remember the searing laser beams?). The fourth is my instant of patience where I finalize my balance and posture, the fifth where my weight increases and the new turn begins in earnest (where my skis cut more deeply into the snow).[14] Figure 22 approximates the corresponding top down view of pelvis, leg and foot from mid transition to early in the turn.

Figure 21. Transition and entering the new turn, continued from Figure 19, with images placed side by side for viewing purposes. Tilt and aim control in action: note the minimum of snow flying during the transition (first four images) which confirms my success at changing the tilt of my skis while keeping them sliding cleanly lengthwise, tails tracking tips.

---

[14] I usually change the tilt of my skis and then aim my feet to match the direction they choose in response. I only override the skis' chosen direction if I want slow or control my speed, by pivoting my feet to force my skis into a skid.

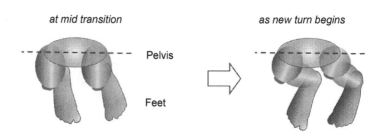

at mid transition   *as new turn begins*

Pelvis

Feet

Figure 22. Looking down at my legs and feet, from mid-transition where I weigh very little, to the start of the new turn where my weight begins to increase. Views correspond to the second and fifth images in Figure 21.

TIP "*Lead with the knees*"

Turn your knees *ever so slightly* into the next turn sooner rather than later, and turn them more when you want your next turn to have a tight radius. You want time to establish balance and posture on suitably tilted skis before any real deflection (and weight increase) begins—turning your knees earlier rather than later gives you more time to prepare a balanced stance on a solid edge grip. Welcome to living on the edge!

From earlier (in **Balance before the turn**), my leg turn during the transition results in my torso facing 'outside' the direction of my skis by the time my mass and line of travel start getting deflected in the new turn. As my weight increases with the turn, bending forward at the hip joints accentuates the tilt of my skis and helps concentrate my weight on my outside boot. Being patient before the deflection and weight increase in the turn gives me a brief instant to fine-tune my balance and posture so I am fully ready when the turn arrives.

Figure 23 shows the instant of patience where I fine-tune balance and posture—with my skis tilted for the upcoming turn while my torso faces in line with momentum—then where my weight increases, my torso just beginning to get turned as deflection begins (more on rotational flow in the next section).

Patience: confirm
balance and posture

Torso faces outside skis by
the time weight increases

Figure 23. Images here show a brief instant of patience to fine-tune balance
and posture before the turn, then weight increasing as the turn begins. Note
the change in direction of the skis under the torso, while the torso stays
facing its momentum-driven direction.

INSIGHT   The natural tendency when learning to ski is to
swivel the upper body in order to twist or pivot the skis left and
right like windshield wipers so they skid and slow our speed with
each turn. Turning the legs without involving the upper body, and
without pivoting the feet with so much force that they override
where the skis want to track allows the skis to provide a stable
platform on which we can balance while they change direction
predictably and gradually under us. The upper body riding, rather
than otherwise moving, rotating or tipping into different positions,
and the feet turning to match our skis' desired path based on tilt,
pressure and bend, rather than trying to overrule where our skis
want to slide, simplifies our act of balancing and makes for more
enjoyable, balanced, flowing skiing.

"It's our job to balance, and our skis' job to turn."

Letting momentum drive my switch leads to balance and flow through the transition and into the next turn. The momentum of my feet and skis carries my feet across under my upper body while the momentum of my upper body carries it towards the inside of the next turn. With momentum producing the change in my body's orientation, I can soften the tension in my legs and core while I flow into a suitable posture for the upcoming turn.

Especially at speed, I feel an upward boost as my switch begins, whether from the virtual hump effect or from a real bump, which leads to a temporary lightweight feeling. While I am light in weight, I can move quickly and relatively easily to prepare my balance and posture for the new turn. This gives me an instant—*before the new turn begins in earnest*—to balance patiently with legs turned, weight centered mostly on the outside foot, and posture ready for the upcoming increase in weight. With these elements intact, my skis enter the turn as predicted and I enjoy a smooth ride through the turn without needing to make any corrective moves. *The delight of riding a big weight change from light to heavy to light while feeling balanced throughout is a real motivator to 'nail it' every turn!*

Figure 24 summarizes the leg movements and pressure changes from turn to turn as discussed in recent sections.

TIP   *"If you need to brake do it early"*

The time to initiate braking to control or check speed is during the transition. This is when my skis are lightly pressured and quite flat on the snow, so are easy to pivot into a skid. Furthermore, I am already turning my legs to prepare for the next turn—so if I'm going to pivot my skis now is the time. Doing so as part of going into the turn is far better than going into the turn too fast on aggressively tilted skis then being unable to deal with the forces or terrain that await me later in the turn. If you want to slow yourself, pivot your skis *before and into* the turn, that is, before deflection and heavier weight make it difficult to do so.

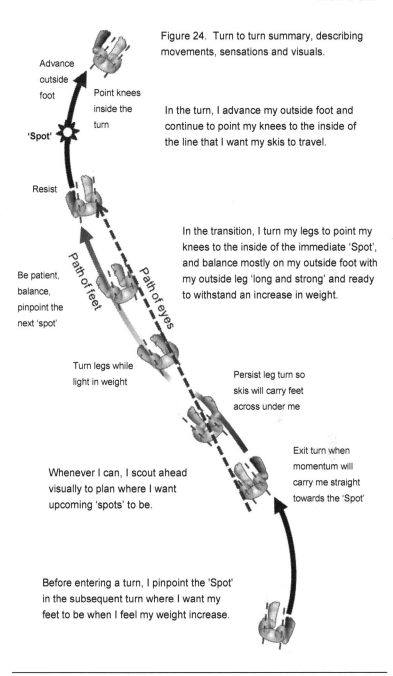

Figure 24. Turn to turn summary, describing movements, sensations and visuals.

Advance outside foot

Point knees inside the turn

'Spot'

Resist

In the turn, I advance my outside foot and continue to point my knees to the inside of the line that I want my skis to travel.

Be patient, balance, pinpoint the next 'spot'

Path of feet

Path of eyes

In the transition, I turn my legs to point my knees to the inside of the immediate 'Spot', and balance mostly on my outside foot with my outside leg 'long and strong' and ready to withstand an increase in weight.

Turn legs while light in weight

Persist leg turn so skis will carry feet across under me

Whenever I can, I scout ahead visually to plan where I want upcoming 'spots' to be.

Exit turn when momentum will carry me straight towards the 'Spot'

Before entering a turn, I pinpoint the 'Spot' in the subsequent turn where I want my feet to be when I feel my weight increase.

What to try

Find a groomed run where your skis can arc turns without picking up too much speed. You should feel extra weight during each turn as your skis arc cleanly without slowing down.

Late in each turn, choose a spot on the snow that is straight ahead of your line of travel. Let your upper body go towards that spot, while keeping enough turn in your legs so your skis, for an instant, continue along their own trajectory. You may sense the snow rising as you let momentum take over and your switch begins (the virtual hump). Resist the hump just enough so you feel light for a good portion of the distance to the spot that you chose.

While you feel light, turn your legs to point your knees to the inside of the spot. *Be sure to not affect or change the direction of your feet when turning your thighs.* Let your skis arc while you balance on your outside ski. As soon as you feel balanced, begin resisting the forces of the new turn.

You should experience a smooth ride and steady view of the upcoming terrain from turn to turn. You should also find that your skis track cleanly and reliably into each turn since you are allowing them to establish their grip and line of travel (which also means you are balanced) before they get pressured by the weight of the turn.

TIP 'to boost your flow'

- Let momentum drive the switch
- Turn thighs to move knees across skis by mid transition
- Take an instant of patience to finalize balance and posture
- Enter the turn with legs and feet turned so torso faces outside the direction of the skis, outside leg long (but not straight), and torso tilted slightly forward from hip joints (no twisting)
- To slow, pivot feet and skis while light in weight and skid into the turn—the snow you throw will slow you down

Upper body tracks momentum

Just as I need to balance atop forces that rise up through my feet, I also need to 'balance' rotationally with forces that spiral up through my feet. *My skis induce a rotational force on me whenever they change direction under me.*

Between turns my feet and skis turn relative to my pelvis and upper body (as in Figure 22) while my mass travels a straight line—here there are no deflection forces at play and gravity offers negligible effect over short periods of time. My upper body facing in line with momentum during the transition provides a helpful directional reference while I turn my legs and guide my skis into the next turn.

During each turn, deflection and rotational forces are at play. Where in the turn these forces peak depends on the length of the turn. In short turns and moguls, they peak briefly mid to late in the turn. In long turns, they begin as soon as my line of travel begins to curve. In any case, the key is to resist or assist any rotational forces just enough that my upper body faces directly in line with momentum at all times—so whenever I exit a turn my upper body will face squarely with its momentum and thus its direction of travel until the next turn begins.[15]

Throughout, *I keep my hip joints and ankles free enough that I can 'pilot' my skis with my lower body while my upper body tracks its line of momentum.* The result: my upper body gets rotated in response to, and slightly lagging to, a change in the line of travel that my skis carry my feet along.[16] See Figure 25.

---

[15] The more a turn changes the direction of my line of travel, the more effort I contribute to ensure my upper body always faces in line with momentum. I accordingly add to or resist the rotation that my skis induce upwards.

[16] Note: I never want my spine twisted to accommodate a difference in the direction of my skis and torso. To avoid this, I turn my legs so my feet can aim along the path of my skis while my pelvis and shoulders remain comfortably in line with each other. This helps me handle heavy weight during turns without risking injury due to a loaded, twisted spine.

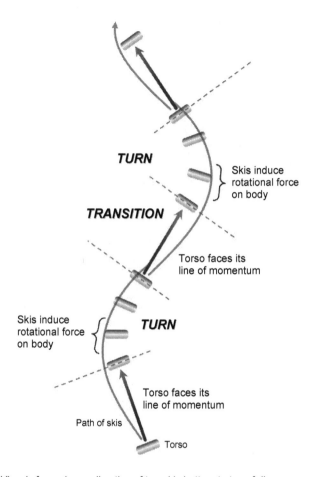

View is from above; direction of travel is bottom to top of diagram

Figure 25. Rotational forces occur during each turn. I resist or assist these forces so my upper body faces its line of momentum at all times. This leads to my upper body facing its (virtually straight) line of travel during each transition. My upper body aligned with its momentum and path of travel is optimal for a strong and balanced entry to the next turn.

My body gets turned while my skis change my line of travel. Look for the relationship of the outside arm (left arm) to the torso. Where does my upper body get turned? Answer: at the apex of the turn, at the third to the fourth image. Note that the torso faces outside of where the skis point, lagging their change in direction.

INSIGHT   Facing one's challenges

My upper body always facing my line of momentum carries two inherent benefits. One, I can exit a turn at any time without needing to turn my upper body to face where it is headed (it already faces straight towards where it will be when the next turn begins). Two, my upper body facing where my weight will increase next makes it easier to get fully prepared (and 'ready to face'...) whatever awaits me in the next turn. Both aspects help me link turns smoothly while descending variable terrain and snow conditions.

What to try

To test your rotational balance hold your poles loosely between thumb and forefinger so they are free to pendulum, and ski fast enough for your skis to arc turns but still slow enough (with little enough wind resistance) that your poles can hang near straight down.

With each turn let your torso rotate as influenced by the forces acting up through your feet. Seek the right amount of tension or effort in your core so the tip of your outside pole swings smoothly forward throughout each turn and into position for planting just after you let momentum take you into the transition.

When successful, your torso will both face and travel straight towards where it will be at the start of the next turn, without needing a heavy pole plant to halt its rotation. Be sure to keep your hands and arms steady relative to your torso so the swing of your poles is due only to the rotational forces arising from your skis, rather than 'cheater' moves with your hands or arms.

Steady the hands

My hands and poles help me balance. *I keep my hands where I can see them in the lower corners of my goggles*—about where I'd want them when walking along a narrow log. In each turn I drag my inside pole tip lightly along the snow to help sense how my body is oriented relative to the hill. What I feel up through my hand and arm complements other balance inputs—sensations from boots, muscle tension in legs, core, neck, and jaw, and the integrated input from eyes and inner ears. Dragging my pole tip also helps me detect balance and rotation issues early so I can make corrections before real trouble develops.

I plant my pole or touch it lightly on the snow at mid transition (at speed, just after the virtual hump). *The result I want from my pole plant is to leave my upper body facing its line of momentum for the rest of the transition.* I plant with whatever force is needed to suit this objective. The amount of force relates to how well balanced I am at the exit of the turn. If I am well balanced, I use more of a touch than a firm plant. If I need to rebalance, rotationally or otherwise, I use a firmer plant.[17]

Seeking no more than a light touch of the pole encourages me to concentrate on balance and to use only my legs to adjust the tilt and aim of my skis. **Steady hands and a light touch of the poles contribute to a calm and quiet upper body and good balance**.

INSIGHT   **Smaller arm movements = simpler to balance.**

During each turn, I guide the tip of my outside pole forward smoothly during the turn so it is poised and ready to plant as I exit the turn. To accommodate the changing angle of my pole I flex my wrist, rather than move my arm relative to my torso. Being centered and balanced when I exit the turn I can easily plant or touch my pole tip with only a small movement of my forearm. After planting or touching my pole tip to the snow, I let my wrist flex—rather than drop my hand—as I ski past where my pole contacted the snow.

What to try

Do slow rhythmic turns along a gentle groomed run. Practice planting your pole tips lightly with each turn using a minimum of arm movement. Rely on flexing mainly the wrist while smoothly easing your outside pole tip forward throughout each turn, then to allow the pole tip (or basket) to swing backwards as you ski past where you planted it. Especially, do not drop your hand after planting the pole. Keep your hands positioned so you can see them in the periphery of your vision throughout turn and transition. **TIP:** Hold your poles lightly—*a white-knuckled grip is not required!*

---

[17] A fun challenge to test how balanced you are at the end of your turns is to ski moguls without poles (park your poles at the top of the hill for full commitment!). You'll find skiing moguls without poles to be quite easy if you are well balanced at the end of each turn, difficult if you're not.

How I Ski

Balance is *'king'* *(and, it's good for the sole...!)*

My 'bottom line' in skiing is ***perfect balance throughout turn and transition***. Skiing in balance is much more efficient and takes far less effort and energy than continually trying to get balanced *(skiing need not be a series of controlled falls and recoveries!)*. I want my skiing to be efficient so I can enjoy the most effective turns possible for a given amount of effort. Perfect balance throughout turn and transition as my core pursuit gives me that efficiency: I can ski more turns, more runs, and more days—and have the most fun possible.

To keep my balancing efforts as simple as possible I ***use only my legs to initiate all adjustments to my skis***, balancing atop the forces that arise through my feet. To keep my skiing as efficient as possible I look ahead to plan the line I want to travel, seek to balance in a suitable posture before each turn begins, and let momentum take over to transition towards the next turn. Throughout turn and transition, I seek a smooth ride and a steady view of the upcoming terrain. I look ahead to plan and predict my line then adapt as required to achieve it.

Relaxation: the corollary of balance

If I am balanced, I can stabilize my body atop the forces I feel up through my feet using the least effort possible.

Minimizing the effort required to stabilize maximizes the muscle available to ski. When I'm balanced and relaxed it's easier to be athletic, to edge and aim the skis, absorb variations in the snow, and achieve and recover balance. I try to relax whatever muscles I don't need to tense, seeking to maintain a balanced, ski-ready posture while using as few muscles with as little tension as possible.

When I feel relaxed while skiing smoothly, I am indeed balanced.

My 'Building Blocks' of Expert Skiing

"Legs turn, torso rides"
Turn thighs and legs to adjust
tilt and aim of the skis

"Balance before the turn"
Patience: balance with
legs turned relative to pelvis,
slight forward bend at hip joints

"Advance feet in the turn"
Draw feet back during the transition,
move them ahead during the turn

"Momentum drives the switch"
Let momentum take the feet across
under the upper body while it
floats (or flies) between turns

"Upper body tracks momentum"
Keep torso tilted forward, as relaxed as
possible, facing in line with momentum,
hands out to the front and sides

"Relax, balance, and enjoy the view"
Keep hands quiet, drag inside pole tip,
relax shoulders and upper back, and
seek a smooth ride with a smooth view

"Predict, adapt and achieve"
Look ahead, use wide angle view to plan, narrow
angle to predict, then adapt to achieve as predicted

4 Key Postures and Movements

In terms of body mechanics, I see alpine skiing as *a sport of dynamic standing.* When skiing, we move athletically through skiing-related postures while we balance on our feet, our movements timed with the forces we feel acting upwards from the snow and through our feet. Figure 26 shows typical postures that we move through while skiing, one posture to the next usually taking but a split second.

Unlike in many other sports and in everyday living, where we use our feet and legs to propel ourselves along a stationary surface, in skiing we get propelled by invisible forces along a surface that feels anything *but* stationary. Rather than powering ourselves from point A to point B, our task becomes adjusting our skis and balancing on them while gravity and momentum propel us from point A to point B along a varying—and at times a very lively—surface.[18]

Most movements involved in expert skiing are already common in everyday living—we only need to learn to apply them to the act of skiing. More challenging are a few that are unusual, even quite unnatural, to everyday living and therefore unlikely to be discovered through trial and error (with the accompanying frustration and pain). Fortunately, standing provides a familiar reference for explaining and understanding such movements.

Earlier I described the building blocks of my skiing. In this section, I describe the key postures and movements that I use and how to practice them. Note that each can be practiced not only on the hill, but *anywhere*—at an airport, in a kitchen, in front of a TV—so they can be familiar and ready to be applied the next time you are skiing.

Please note that the descriptions here are to help you understand and familiarize with skiing-related postures and movements, rather than to outline a substitute for ski fitness exercises.

---

[18] We 'feel the earth ...move ...under our feet'. Fortunately, no tumbling down occurs, unless we lose control...

Alpine skiing ~

"a sport of dynamic standing"

Figure 26. Skiing is a sport of dynamic standing, in which we balance on our feet while the surface under us heaves and bounces. We also get to travel, gravity-powered, through beautifully scenic places, sometimes at exciting speeds. It's a great experience truly *worth living for!*

Ready = centered, relaxed, and flex-able

I use a reference posture called the 'ready position'. My ready position has *my weight centered and muscles relaxed other than to stabilize myself in a ski-ready posture from which I can flex in any direction*.

In the ready position I,

- Feel pressure from my boot cuffs equally against my shins and calves (when not in boots, my kneecaps are over the balls of my feet)
- Feel equal weight on each foot, equally shared by forefoot and heel (the 'centerpoint' under the tibia)
- Stand with knees bent so when viewed from the side, the angle of my thighs mirrors that of my shins
- Bend at my hip joints to where glancing down I see along my shins to the entire tops of my boots (or feet) from the ankles forwards
- Hold my hands equally ahead and to the side where I see them in my peripheral vision, placed such that my elbows are in the same vertical plane as my knees, and (on hill) my pole tips rest beside my toes
- Head balanced over spine, upper back and shoulder muscles relaxed, eyes looking slightly upwards and straight ahead (peering through the top half of my goggles).

What to try

To practice the ready position at home, stand with your toes about a foot from the face of a kitchen cabinet and your knees over the balls of your feet (roughly where they'll be in ski boots). Reach your hands equally forward and out to the side, near the edge of the countertop. Balance your head where you can relax your neck muscles, then bend at the hip joints (but not your waist!) enough so that when you glance down—without craning your neck—you see along your shins to the whole tops of your feet. Finally, adjust the bend in your knees and hips until you feel the same weight on each foot, shared equally between forefoot and heel. When in ski boots, stand so you feel equal pressure from your boot cuffs on your shins and calves. See Figure 27.

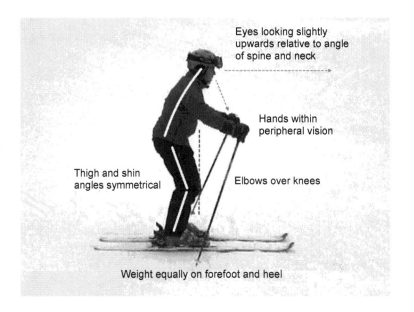

Figure 27. My 'safe haven' ready position, which I move through at mid transition. Different situations will encourage more bend at hips and knees.

From this 'safe haven' position I can flex in any direction. I can bend or straighten at my hips, knees, and ankles (albeit my ankle flex will be minimal when restricted by my ski boots). I can flex sideways, or laterally, at the same primary joints. And, I can turn my thighs—with or without turning my feet—to point my knees to the left or right of where my pelvis and torso face.

When skiing, I flow through the ready position at mid transition, with variations to the standing-at-rest posture above depending on the situation. The variations include more bend at the knees and hips if I want to be small (such as having just absorbed the virtual hump or a real bump), and, feet turned to be in line with my skis as they cross under my upper body en route to the next turn. The following images show several examples of the ready position while skiing.

Examples of the 'safe haven' ready position in various skiing situations. Uppers: cruising and carving. Lower left: moguls, lower right: steeps. Note that the feet are generally turned a little relative to my pelvis and upper body when skiing. This is because they are following my skis as they cross under me, rather than being straight ahead as shown in the practice position in Figure 27.

Turn legs (thighs only)

The foremost move in my skiing (and quite unnatural in everyday life) is *turning my legs without turning or tilting my pelvis, and without (necessarily) turning my feet*. I turn my legs relative to my pelvis, and use my feet and ankles to fine-tune the amount of tilt and aim I want to transmit to my skis. Using the same muscles to turn my thighs for both tilt and aim control ensures that whatever adjustment I make to my skis is done with strength. Further, avoiding active shifting around of the upper body minimizes upsetting or challenging my balance. Figure 28 illustrates my leg moves.

Views looking down at feet

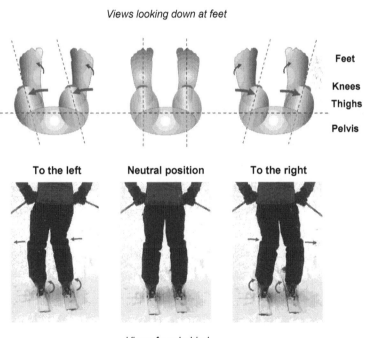

Feet

Knees

Thighs

Pelvis

| To the left | Neutral position | To the right |

Views from behind

Figure 28. Tilt control: turning legs (when slightly bent) without turning pelvis or feet. Use effort in the big muscles to turn thighs, point knees and edge skis. Your feet will naturally roll as you do so; you should feel your weight move side-to-side accordingly on the soles of your feet.

Turning the legs to tilt the skis relative to the body, or, to 'edge' the skis.
Compare the turn of the outside leg in the first and third images here with
the lower left and lower right images in Figure 28.

INSIGHT   You don't need to turn your legs 'big'; a few degrees
will do. *The key is to move freely at the hip joints.* Isolation of the
turning of your legs from the influence of your upper body is what's
important to achieve 'separation' between upper and lower body. To
borrow an expression, "it's not the size, it's the movement" that
counts. Or, at a stretch, thighs *DOES* matter...

What to try

Turning the legs independently of your pelvis is a move you can practice anywhere, anytime, depending on the company you keep (i.e., high tolerance to witnessing silly-looking moves).

Stand with knees slightly bent and hands on hips. **Turn both legs in unison** to point your knees left and right **without letting your pelvis or feet change direction**. Let your feet roll or tilt side to side as you turn your legs but don't let them change direction. You can also do this exercise with ski boots on, and with skis on. Of course with skis on and sliding downhill, you will quickly realize that you are skiing!

HINT: to feel the leg muscles that work to edge your skis, stand on a carpet in sock feet as in the "ready position" in Figure 27. Pretend to unscrew a giant bottle cap that is under your right foot—balance mostly on your right foot and turn your whole leg to the left (keep your pelvis steady!) so your arch stays in one place, and your toes and heel scrub the carpet with each turn of your leg. After ten or so repeats you should feel the appropriate muscles. Be sure to perform the mirrored equivalent to familiarize for your left leg (screw the giant bottle cap back into place—make sure it's tight!).

TIP   **Hold those hips steady**   When turning thighs to point knees, it is very important to resist the urge to rotate the pelvis (and hips) to drive the knees sideways or forwards. Hands on the hips can help to keep the pelvis steady and facing straight ahead.

A Hunch?   When carving skis first emerged, I heard anecdotes about people (relatively good skiers) developing sore knees due to the 'new' skis being so reactive and 'turny'. I have a hunch that these people were untrained at turning their legs—when their skis turned under them it created a twisting stress to their knees and led to soreness. Try this: standing, point both feet to the left or right, towards 10 or 2 o'clock or thereabouts. Now, without moving your feet, press your knees straight ahead towards 12 o'clock to mimic skis turning under bent but non-turning legs...more than a hunch perhaps?

On snow, I practice turning *only my legs* while skiing along gentle groomed slopes or roads. I'll alternate between standing on one leg and then two legs at a time (see the second *What to try* in **Legs turn, torso rides** in chapter 3, *Techniques in Motion*). This exercise is a great way to use time productively while sliding along otherwise long and tedious mind-numbing run outs.

Flex vertically over a steady centerpoint

When skiing, the terrain often rises and falls under me, particularly in moguls. Even on smooth groomed runs, when I'm traveling fast enough to arc turns, the snow feels like it rises then falls during each transition (the "virtual hump" effect). To ski well I need to accommodate changes in the distance between my torso and the snow *and keep balanced while doing so*.

My approach is to absorb the rise and fall of the snow by bending at my knees and hip joints while keeping the weight distribution on the soles of my feet constant.[19]

My natural tendency when flexing vertically in everyday situations, such as when bending down to lift something, is to bend at my ankles, knees and hips, and let my weight momentarily shift forward a little towards my toes. If I did the same while skiing—when my lower legs are clamped into stiff boots—any forward bend in my ankles would mash my shins into the cuffs of my boots. My boots being stiff and somewhat elastic would then rebound, springing my skis ahead, my torso upright, and me into the dreaded 'back seat'.[20]

---

[19] The amount of pressure I feel from underfoot may change, but my goal is to have where I feel it on the soles of my feet remain steady.

[20] Getting bounced 'into the back seat' is a precursor to getting tossed 'out the back door', an easy expression to identify with if you've ever smacked the back of your head on the hill after falling backwards out of a turn (ouch!!).

To avoid this unsettling rebound I try to bend only at my hips and knees, and little if any at my ankles. My ankles flex a little anyways—I can't freeze them at a particular angle (they aren't that strong). Further, I don't consciously bend my spine or neck—I want them in a neutral position so they are positioned to flex a little while I ride over bumps and ripples. Figure 29 illustrates how I move to flex vertically.

Let head tilt with spine to reduce neck strain

Hands reach forward to help stay balanced over centerpoint

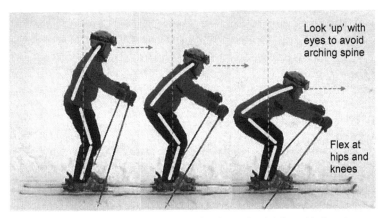

Look 'up' with eyes to avoid arching spine

Flex at hips and knees

Weight steady on forefoot and heel, no change in ankle bend

Figure 29. Flexing vertically without challenging our balance.
Keep how your boots feel against your shins and calves and the soles of your feet ***steady and unchanging while you bend and extend***.

Whether absorbing real bumps or the virtual hump, my goal is to shorten and extend my body without changing where my weight is centered. If I can leave one turn and enter the next without feeling pressure spikes on my shins or calves, goal achieved!

What to try

Flexing vertically is another movement you can practice in mixed company—if you can shoulder questioning comments and inquisitive looks.

Start in the ready position and *lower your hips towards the floor about 6 to 8 inches without flexing your ankles, and without changing how your weight feels on the soles of your feet*.

No flexing of the ankles simulates wearing ski boots. Being practiced at flexing only at the hips and knees will reduce the tendency to push your shins forward onto your boot cuffs, and then need to deal with the problems that causes. When practicing *in ski boots aim to feel constant pressure on your shins and calves, and constant pressure on the soles of your feet, while you bend and extend*. Whether or not you are wearing ski boots, be sure to reach your arms well forward to help keep your weight centered as you bend.

One final point: keep your eyes trained ahead on a distant spot (remember: *Look ahead to improve your balance*) as you flex lower. Look 'up' with your eyes rather than by arching your back or neck to hold your head up. This will help you relax and avoid awkward, soreness-inducing positions.

Flex laterally – within a range of strength

Flexing laterally helps me control the tilt of my skis and thus my lateral balance, and the shape of my turns. From earlier, the tilt on my skis is primarily set by the orientation of my internal barbell. I fine-tune the amount of tilt on my skis by 'edging'—which I do by flexing laterally.

To flex laterally I turn my legs (with knees bent a little) without turning my pelvis or feet. I allow the bend in my hip joints to increase as the weight of the turn squeezes me into a classic mid-turn skier posture. Flexing laterally relies on mobility in several joints. Rotational flex in the ankle allows my foot and ski to turn a little compared to the turn of my leg. This allows the skis to follow their preferred line through the transition while I turn my legs and prepare for the new turn (review Figure 12, in **Balance before the turn**). Rotational flex in the hip sockets produces an appearance of a sideways bend at the knees, more so with more knee bend.[21] Lateral and forward flex at the hip joints allows my upper legs (thighs and femurs) to move side to side under my pelvis, so I *achieve a lateral flex that helps 'edge' my skis without any sideways bend in my spine*. See Figure 30 for more clarity.

When viewed from in front or behind, my body appears curved sideways when I bend laterally. *The amount of lateral bend is a tradeoff between adding tilt to my skis and maintaining a posture that can withstand my weight in a turn.* With the possibility of heavy weight during turns, I bend mostly at my hip joints and knees—and leave my spine and neck neutral and able to flex a little if required.

Being familiar with flexing laterally allows me to tilt my skis smoothly, and to know how far I can flex before stressing muscles, ligaments or joints. I practice moving through my full range of lateral bending to mimic the smoothness I want while skiing.

---

[21] The knees don't actually bend sideways. Rotational flex in the hip joints and ankles produces the illusion of a sideways bend at the knees while the legs are turned relative to the pelvis.

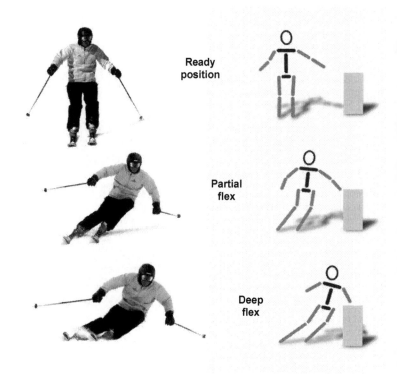

Figure 30. Lateral flexing in action on the hill and in the kitchen (or anywhere with a support at hand). Note the lateral bend at the hip joint allows the pelvis, spine and shoulders (the lighter shaded lines on the right) to hold their position relative to each other while the flex deepens.

INSIGHT "Bend at the waist" is a common misnomer for "bend at the hip joints" (the latter being more accurate, though awkward to say). My hip is designed to hold a lot of weight when my thigh is anywhere within quite a wide range of angles relative to my pelvis. My spine isn't able to hold a lot of weight while hunched, arched, or bent sideways. Being averse to pain, I bend at the hip joints—not at the waist—and keep my spine neutral so it is in position to flex with the inevitable forces of skiing.

What to try

Flexing laterally is easy enough to practice as long as you have a support handy, say a countertop or wall, that you can lean on (otherwise, you'll end up lying on the floor). This move is something that people typically associate with skiing so even the testiest onlookers should remain thankfully silent.

Start in the ready position with your hand a few inches away from a sturdy support. ***Without turning your pelvis, turn both legs to point your knees and feet a little towards the support*** (to one o'clock if the support is to your right)—this leaves your pelvis and torso facing to the 'outside' of where your feet and skis point without having rotated your upper body. Now slowly 'slide' your torso sideways, without tilting it or rotating it, using your outstretched hand for support. Take the weight off your foot that is nearer the support (the 'inside' foot) so most of your weight rests on the arch side of your other foot (the 'outside' foot). Flex deeply, bending at the hip joints and knees, sharing your weight between the arch side of your 'outside' foot and your hand. Keep your shoulders, spine and pelvis in the same position relative to each other as you flex.

You should reach a position where your lower legs are at a significant angle to your torso (a much greater angle than you'll want on the hill). Flex as deeply as is comfortable without straining anything, being careful to avoid turning your pelvis. Move slowly between the starting and deepest flex positions to develop control and to familiarize with different amounts of flex. Repeat the above while facing in the opposite direction (being able to turn both ways will come in handy once on hill…).

Note: ***when skiing, our legs and feet need to be free to turn independently to the direction of our pelvis***. To simulate this, start with your legs and feet turned *away* from the support (to eleven o'clock if the support is to your right). *While you slide your torso sideways turn your legs and feet* so they point to one o'clock by the time your hand contacts the support. When skiing, the feet change direction to the pelvis in a similar manner during the transition, reaching their turn-ready direction just before the new turn begins.

One final note: a flexed mid-turn position when skiing is much more comfortable than during this routine, since when skiing we are balanced on our outside foot rather than suspended between its arch and the opposite hand. (See the upcoming section.)

Hip joint 'over' centerpoint

At mid-turn, I balance mostly on my outside foot. My outside leg is relatively straight and when viewed from in front or behind, my outside hip joint appears in line with or 'over' my centerpoint. My core is engaged to hinge forward at the hip joints (to advance my feet in the turn) yet not hinge so much that I collapse under the weight of the turn.

I can mimic a mid turn posture when stationary to practice the relative position of torso and limbs and approximate a mid turn sensation. I find it helpful to picture a balancing scale (like the 'scales of justice') with the fulcrum where my outside leg attaches to its hip joint. One side of the scale carries the weight of my inside arm, leg, boot and ski, which is counterbalanced by the weight of my head, outside shoulder, and outside arm, at least when I'm doing my turns justice.[22] See Figure 31.

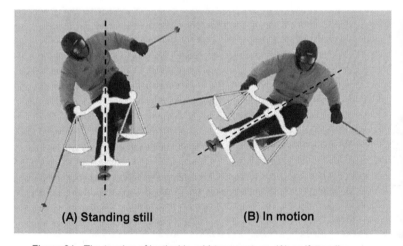

(A) Standing still　　　　**(B) In motion**

Figure 31. The 'scales of justice' in mid-turn posture, (A) as if standing still and balanced in line with gravity only, and (B) when in motion and balanced atop the combined forces of gravity and deflection. The outside hip joint acts as the fulcrum of the scale in the lateral direction.

---

[22] I bet you saw that one coming...

My upper body balanced on the ball joint of my outside hip allows me to hold my ski at a significant tilt and still withstand heavy turning forces. My outside leg stays relatively straight in order to withstand my heavier weight during an aggressive arc turn. The lateral bend at my hip joint helps achieve a high tilt angle on my ski yet allows me to keep my spine neutral, and positioned suitably for heavy loads.[23]

Moving between a ready position and a one-footed mid turn posture while standing stationary helps to familiarize with the mid turn position and how it feels (albeit while skiing we weigh more due to deflection forces plus gravity). Practicing this position also helps to ensure that come time to ski we will have a leg to stand on.[24]

What to try

This is something that you might not want to practice with others around—it may elicit too many questioning stares and distracting comments.

Start in the ready position, torso tilted forward at the hip joints. Place your thumbs on your lower ribs and your fingertips on your pelvic bone. Slowly lift one foot, the one on the 'inside' of the turn, and at the same time bend laterally at your hip joint to tilt your upper body to the 'outside' of the turn. Continue tilting your upper body until your raised foot approaches knee height. **Keep the distance from your thumbs to your fingertips constant—bend only at the hip joint of your outside leg; avoid bending sideways using your spine.** Experiment with how far you can flex the hip joint without bending your spine, and how turning your leg (and foot) slightly to the 'inside' of the turn allows you to bend the hip joint farther. Extend your arms to complete the picture, being sure to keep your scales of justice in equilibrium (meaning don't fall over). Repeat a few times then switch legs.

---

[23] Rotational flex in the hip joint allows the thighs to turn which produces an apparent lateral bend at the hip joint and knee, and lateral flex in the hip joint allows the femur to move to the side to produce a true lateral bend at the hip joint. Notably, *my spine doesn't need to bend sideways to my pelvis in order to achieve a lateral bend of my body.*

[24] Hah!

> **INSIGHT** What posture allows you to resist the weight of the turn, yet hold your skis tilted sufficiently relative to the direction that your weight acts downwards through them in order to produce a solid edge grip while your skis turn under you? Each of us is built a little differently, but for me that strongest position has my upper body
> (a) facing a little to the outside of where my feet point,
> (b) tilted forward by flexing at the hip joints, and
> (c) balanced over a long and strong outside leg that is turned inwards at an angle to my pelvis.

Spine neutral and tilted forward

Since skiing generates significant loads on my body, I want my spine positioned to deal with such loads. When I lift a heavy object, I avoid twisting and bending my spine while reaching to lift and during the lift (just like in worker safety manuals)—*I never want to twist my spine (shoulders turned relative to pelvis) or bend laterally using my spine (shoulders tilted relative to pelvis).* My spine will flex a little in both aspects under the forces of skiing, but I avoid consciously twisting or bending it in pursuit of a good skiing posture.

I ski with my torso tilted a little forward as in the ready position, or even a little more, so if I glance down I can see both the toe and arch buckles of my boots. Having my torso tilted forward positions me to absorb rises and falls in terrain without stressing my back or neck unnecessarily.[25]

Figure 32 shows the forward angle of my torso relative to my legs that is typical at late turn.

---

[25] I've seen skiers with legs braced, torso vertical and spine hunched, their head craned forward and their neck bobbing like a fishing rod that has hooked a real fighter. Very painful looking!! I keep a few of my favorite physiotherapist's business cards on hand just for these people...

Figure 32. Typical posture mid-to-late in the turn. Note the amount of forward bend at the hip joints, which isn't apparent in the front view of Figure 31.

The forward tilt of my upper body as shown in Figure 32 means I am ready to bend as I travel over bumps and rises. If I were to ski with my torso vertical, a rise in terrain would move my feet ahead of my torso (by virtue of my boots not letting my ankles bend very much), triggering the notorious 'in the back seat' foible. Alternatively, if I forced my shins forward into my boot cuffs to keep my feet under me I'd get nasty rebound and a rough ride. A rough ride, besides challenging my balance, would jostle my head and compromise my ability to see well, perpetuating a fight to stay upright.

INSIGHT   I don't want to 'waste' any available flex in my spine to simply stand in a ready posture. Generally, I want my spine neutral and thus able to flex in any direction so I am better able to deal with rises and dips in the snow. In particular, I avoid skiing with my back hunched forward (though I've been instructed to do so many times). I also never try to "feel the pinch" between my rib cage and pelvis by bending sideways in the spine, contrary to instruction to do so (I happily admit that I don't understand the 'illogic' of this contortion). Focusing on bending at the hip joints keeps spine flex in reserve to help me deal with the heaving surface under my feet with a minimum risk of hurt.

How I Ski

Figure 33 shows 'upright' or 'hunched' postures that I avoid and the 'ready' posture that I use. Bending primarily with the hip joints and knees reduces the odds of both immediate and long term discomfort in the back and neck. 'Upright' leaves fore and aft balance precarious since it eliminates one of our two primary bending options (the hip joints)—something has got to give and it is usually balance. 'Hunched' in my experience is a surefire shortcut to neck and back pain. I find that actively bending at the hips and knees and leaving my spine to flex as needed is comfortable and allows my back to get stronger, rather than sorer, with skiing.

Figure 33. Two postures I avoid (but have often seen) and the movements I use: bending primary at the hips and knees in order to have some spine flex 'in reserve' for demanding instants.

What to try

**Tilt your upper body forward from the hip joints, and peer
through the upper half of your goggle lenses—rather than
trying to keep your head level.** When practicing this head
position, keep your torso tilted forward at least as much as in your
ready position. A brief glance down should sight along your shins to
the whole tops of your feet without any obstruction by your knees.

Avoid trying to hold your head level at all times since this places
your head in a tilted back position—as when you look skyward—
and when skiing your head craned out on an extended neck can
lead to uncomfortable consequences.

You can check the position of your spine, neck and head against
the above description while sliding straight along a gentle slope or
a road. Flex to lower your upper body towards the snow as
described earlier in "**Flex vertically over a steady centerpoint**".
When doing so, compare the difference in comfort you feel when
you peer through the upper half of your goggles versus arching
your neck and head back in order to keep your gaze through the
middle of your goggles.

Postures and movements to practice (anywhere)

Stand ready
Learn to move quickly into this neutral, flex-able, and balanced 'safe haven'

Turn legs (thighs only)
Turn legs without rotating or tilting pelvis; simplifies act of balancing throughout turn and transition

Flex vertically over centerpoint
Flex at knees and hips while keeping centerpoint steady; helps absorb terrain changes while preserving balance

Flex laterally within strength
Turn legs while retaining rotational freedom in ankles and hip joints (stay within a range of comfort); helps control and hold tilt of skis

Hip joint over centerpoint
Balance on one foot with hip joint in line with centerpoint, body mass balanced on hip joint; helps strong posture and strong edge hold

Spine and neck neutral and tilted forward
Tilt torso forward as in ready position, look through upper half of goggles to avoid hyper extended neck; helps balance and vision

5   Advice for Various Situations and Conditions

Each skiing situation is an opportunity to explore and develop skills, advance your skiing and maximize your fun. I like to have points to focus on in different scenarios to help make skiing easy and enjoyable. Here are a few such points that I find worthwhile exploring in different skiing situations and conditions.

Easy groomers – develop your turns

Easy groomed runs are great for playing with different types of turns. I think in terms of ***three basic turn types: pure arc, skidded carve, and pivoted sliders***. Pure arcs change my direction of travel most effectively and efficiently, achieving a given change in direction within a minimum distance and with a minimum of slowing—great for racing and maintaining speed. The mark of a pure arc turn is two narrow grooves etched in the snow (thus the expression "let's park some arcs!"). Skidded carves achieve a given direction change but at a slower speed or over a greater distance than a pure arc turn will. They also leave wider and shallower grooves in the snow since the skis slip a little sideways throughout the turn, creating friction and braking—great for controlling speed. Pivoted sliders are the least efficient, in terms of effort spent for the change in direction achieved. The skier pivots their skis into a skid and waits for their skis to begin sliding along the direction they are pointed in. Pivoted sliders leave a smear in the snow, or when it is icy, emit a noisy telltale scraping 'grind' as the skis scratch sideways—great for looking bad! Figure 34 depicts the direction change and line of travel that the skis deliver with each type of turn.

Pure arcs

A pure arc turn is created when tilted skis track along the curve of their lengthwise bend, tails exactly following tips. Pressure due to the forces that press up through my boots and deflect my line of travel (and make me feel heavier than normal) helps my skis cut into the snow and execute a smooth arc. The reward: a smooth stable turn that feels wonderful.

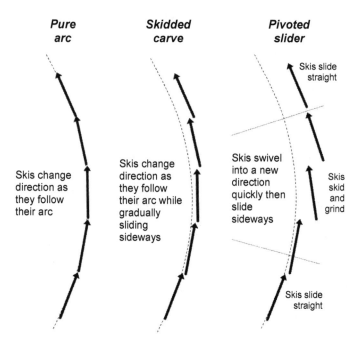

Figure 34. Different turn approaches and results. My line of travel is deflected most effectively by a pure arc turn (along the dashed line).

Skidded carves *("it was a skid...not a pivot!"[26])*

A skidded carve is a pure arc combined with a gradual sideways slip. In a well executed skidded carve my skis change direction on the basis of tilt, pressure and bend, but they are tilted less than enough to produce a pure arc turn. I use skidded carves in many situations since they dissipate energy (through friction and spraying snow sideways to my line of travel) and thus help me control speed. They are also handy when I'm traveling too slowly for my skis to arc cleanly, or, when I want a sharper change in line of travel than a pure arc turn would deliver at my current speed.

---

[26] As from Seinfeld: "...it was a scratch, not a pick!"

Pivoted sliders

A pivoted slider occurs when skis are forced to point in a direction other than that dictated by their tilt, pressure and bend. Pivoting points the skis, then sideways-acting friction given their tilt and pressure determines how quickly the skis begin to slide in the direction they are pointed in. If it is icy, you can hear the skis scrape and grind noisily until their grip eventually wins over momentum and the skier begins to be carried in a new direction. Turn accomplished!

Lose the grind

Easier to spot than Waldo, a less skilled skier is often seen pivoting their skis, usually with a big upper body rotation for extra swivel power, then pushing their skis sideways in order to slow themselves and achieve a semblance of a turn. This takes a lot of effort and can be tiring, though it helps stay warm on a cold day... It takes much less effort to simply tilt the skis and balance on them—using a little leg turning effort—so our skis carry us smoothly (and quietly) into a new direction. **Graduating from pivot and slide to tilt and balance elevates us from 'grind' crew to pilot...**

Aim to help skis carve better

When my skis have difficulty gripping the snow and 'picking up' the line I intend them to carve I guide them by continuously aiming them along the line I expect they should travel based on their tilt, pressure and bend. A little pivoting effort in the direction I want my skis to point in while they turn themselves helps compensate for uneven or unpredictable snow (or not-as-sharp-as-I-wish edges on my skis!). The key is to 'aim' my skis exactly along the line that their tilt, pressure and bend dictate they should travel in at any given instant. Too little pivoting effort and my skis turn slower and less than they should; too much and they end up in a 'pivoted slider'—the skis change direction but my line of travel remains little affected until my skis bite in and start to carry me in their new direction. **Guiding my skis by aiming them along an intended arc improves the edge grip of my skis and the deflection of my line of travel.**

Whatever turn shape you choose, be sure to advance your feet through the turn for optimum balance.

Slow zones – develop your balance

We've all seen these zones, marked by banners and mountain safety people promoting "slowness". While slow skiing lacks the thrill factor, it is cruelly effective at amplifying even the most minor of deficiencies in balance, evidenced by how much correcting we need to do in order to stay feeling centered and balanced. Our boots tell us quite quickly whenever we are in less than perfect balance.[27]

"Learn-in' the BIZ"

Slow zones are "Balance Improvement Zones" in disguise. In these zones, I ski as slowly as my patience permits, seeing how slowly I can ski without needing to correct my balance for my lack thereof. The challenge to skiing slowly is akin to balancing on a bicycle while riding very slowly. As 'painful' as it is, slow speed sharpens my sense of where my feet need to be and how much to ease them forward so they feel exactly 'under' me, maintaining a steady centerpoint throughout each

---

[27] Recalling that our boots help us 'to ski with sole', knowing just how often we get out of balance at the slowest of beats might trigger some blues:
'the thrill is gone... and my balance is too...
nobody loves me 'cept my momma... sometimes I think she's jivin' too...'

turn. It also forces me to aim my skis by turning my legs and feet so my skis track into each turn, tails following tips. This focus on balance and rotational suppleness in the hip joints, legs and feet helps me feel wonderfully balanced when I resume regular speeds.

Balance vs. Balancing

Whereas balance means *being balanced*, balanc*ing* is the act of *trying to get balanced*. The more proficient I am at accurately predicting where my skis will slide—and thus the where my feet will be at any instant—the more time I am likely to spend in balance versus getting into balance. **Being continually in balance allows me to plan my line and then ski it as predicted, rather than to expend effort continuously recovering balance**. Using slow zones to work on balance is a good way to learn what being in balance feels like, and to develop skills related to balancing.

Skiing turns at very slow speeds helps to develop and test balance-while-turning-legs skills. Suggestion: ski as slowly as patience permits (the speed you walk while shopping?) the next time you are in a slow zone.

How I Ski

Carvers – seek flow and efficiency

"Turn your knees, not your skis"

I turn my thighs to point my knees 'inside' of the line I want my skis to travel, then balance while my skis carve or arc their turn. **The critical move is turning my legs without turning my feet and without rotating or tilting my pelvis.** This action lets me adjust the tilt of my skis relative to the orientation of my internal barbell. While turning my outside leg inwards and across my pelvis may be a little unusual in everyday living, the amount of turn is modest and well within a range of strength—at most plus or minus a few minutes imagining that I am standing on a giant clock face. This keeps my legs within a strong range of movement, and able to withstand the increase in weight I feel as my skis arc their turn.

"Progressive and proactive; never static, always active"

To stay mobile and athletic, **I move 'through' rather than 'to' various positions or postures, timing my movement and effort with the changes in weight I feel up through my feet**. Whatever the turn to turn rhythm, I move with that rhythm to and through whatever posture suits each turn. Long turns may take as long as two seconds from apex to apex (heaviest to heaviest), short turns less than a second. Whatever the timing, I seek to make smooth continuous movements that are timed to the changes in upward forces (the weight) I feel from turn to turn.

Perfection: when there's nothing left to take out
(Or, "simplicity is prerequisite to reliability")

I use momentum to help minimize how much I need to contribute to each turn, seeking efficiency in my movements from turn to turn. While momentum drives my switch from one turn to the next, I turn my thighs to control the tilt on my skis, then balance and ride the skis along the turn they deliver. I don't bend my body sideways to help tilt my skis or try to 'push' my skis downwards to add pressure to them (both unnecessary). Mainly I balance and bend forward a little at the hip joints as I get compressed by the force of the turn. **A well executed turn creates a build up of force that compresses my stance into a dynamic-looking bent-skier position in time with the forces of the turn.**

My weight compresses me into a compact posture at the heaviest part of the turn. I avoid moving to this posture earlier than when my increased weight squeezes me there, since proactively bending, tilting, or otherwise moving my upper body around adds complexity to my balancing act.

Short turns – work on timing and feel

By definition, short turns involve some skidding at the apex of the turn since the skis are being asked to turn more sharply than clean arcs would produce. Skidding helps control speed, especially useful on steeper slopes. The key is to be in perfect balance at the apex of each turn where I weigh the most and my line of travel changes the quickest.

Clean, early edge and an instant of patience

Between turns, my switch reorients my body while I turn my legs to add tilt to my skis. For short turns, my leg turn is pronounced and early since the time between turns is brief—my knees cross over my skis very early in the transition. This helps get my skis sliding cleanly along their edges early and gives me an instant to be patient while they establish their track. When the apex arrives, **the skis turn quickly with a little skid that dissipates energy and keeps my speed under control**.

How I Ski

Feel fore aft balance cues

If I balance well in the fore aft direction, I can then concentrate on moves that make my skis turn where and how I want. I monitor my fore-aft balance through the pressure I feel from my boot cuffs against my shins and calves, plus where I feel my weight centered on the soles of my feet. **I prefer equal pressure on shin and calf, but when the going gets tough, slightly more pressure on the shin adds a little safety margin from the 'back seat'.** When my skis are tilted and carving, I feel pressure centered and concentrated along the arch side of my outside foot. I know I'm centered when my skis carve their turn reliably and naturally, and I remain balanced without needing any corrective moves. For backup, I stay ready to use a strong pole plant to help improve or recover my balance between turns.

Short radius turns, with a slight skid at the apex of the turn (third image). These turns are a good warm up for skiing moguls. Note: the images above are spread out whereas in reality they overlap—note the hut in the background (also, see the same sequence as it appeared in action, in **Upper body tracks momentum** just after Figure 25).

Moguls – keep moving and have fun

When one leg is not enough

Some paths through moguls will yield the occasional big compression that is more than one leg can bear. **When I encounter a trough or bump that demands respect, I take the heaviest part of the turn on both feet.** I still aim to feel the majority of weight on my outside foot, which facilitates a smooth exit of the turn and subsequent switch.

'Momma bear's porridge' – not too hot, not too cold

Always strive for 'centricity', able to do a little less or a little more in any given aspect. Examples: turn legs left or right relative to pelvis, add or reduce the degrees of leg turn, bend smaller or extend taller. **Avoid the limits of your range of movement; that is where impending injuries lurk.** Use only postures with good skeletal alignment and flex vertically, laterally or rotationally within a strain-free range.

Plant for balance

When planting poles don't be a spear chucker, throw roundhouse punches, or otherwise reach far with your arms. Some leg flex going into the transition keeps my upper body close to the hill so I can plant my pole with only a minor bob of the hand. I reach my pole tip well down the hill, *more by pointing my pole than by reaching with my arm*. Keeping the movement of my arms to a quiet minimum allows me to use them like a tightrope walker's balance pole. **TIP: Hold your pole loosely enough so it is easy to plant its tip one pole length or more away from your feet without completely straightening your arm.**

Let it pass

The pole plant is usually no more than a light touch on the snow when I have my balance and upper body rotation under control. On groomed runs, my pole plant is usually a light touch since I'm generally in balance. Moguls are more demanding and I may need a little firmer plant to help keep my body in a good orientation. Whether light or heavy, **after planting I let my wrist flex so I can keep my hand steady** rather than letting it drop down as I ski past where my pole tip struck the snow.

Flexing my wrist and minimizing the movement of my arm helps keep my upper body quiet so I can flow smoothly into the next turn.

Out of balance? Turn anyway
Maintaining rhythm is key to skiing moguls. We may not be balanced perfectly with each turn but as long as we are quite balanced, we still have a fraction of a second to halt our fall and keep our head out of the snow. There's no better way to keep our rhythm going than to 'turn anyway'. You may need a stronger than normal pole plant, some pivoting of the skis, or maybe even some upper body rotation to get the skis to change direction and preserve your rhythm. All's fair—just do it soon enough so you maintain your flow and keep on truckin'...and turning.[28]

Skiing moguls puts into action good technique plus athleticism to deal with changes in terrain. The fundamentals of leg turning, advancing feet in the turn, and flexing vertically over a constant centerpoint play prominently in achieving a smooth in-balance flow.

---

[28] Balance may be good for the sole, but rhythm is what keeps us moving...

Powder and steeps – enjoy the variety

Ride the 'magic carpet'

Imagine that you are standing on a small carpet that is just large enough to encircle your bindings. Keeping your feet tidily positioned will make for easier skiing in powder, crud and moguls. When your feet are within this 'magic carpet', they feel right under you rather than somewhere out to the side. Allow some knee bend late in each turn and into the transition to help you control the tilt of your skis (driven by leg turn) and link your flow from one turn to the next.

Aim feet to keep skis parallel

How close should your feet be in powder? Close enough for your skis to provide a flotation platform. You can ski feet together or feet apart, but do ***hold your skis parallel by consciously aiming them both in the same direction***—aim your legs to point your knees and feet and skis. This will keep your skis from splaying or crossing, regardless of the distance between your feet.

Bounce on a fluffy mattress

When floating in powder I feel like I'm bouncing while standing on my skis on a mattress.[29] Each turn corresponds to my skis sinking into the mattress and each transition when they rebound upwards. Different snow conditions deliver a different stiffness of mattress and a different reaction to our bounces. ***The key to skiing powder is determining how strongly and deeply to bounce on our ski-and-snow mattress***. When I ski powder, I begin by sliding straight to gain some speed, bounce once to feel the reaction I get, then bounce thereafter with each turn, letting my switch happen each time my skis rebound. I like my ski tips to plunge with each bounce—this often produces a pleasing face shot (more so the deeper the snow...). Letting my ski tips submerge with each turn also controls my speed (just a little) so I have more time to plan my route, through dips, over bumps and around trees.

---

[29] No, I've never worn my skis to bed...

How I Ski

See the snow or be the tree

When skiing off-piste amidst trees and powdery stashes that are punctuated with stumps and boulders, I **concentrate on where the snow is, rather than where the obstacles are**. My thinking is it's better to look where I want to travel, and avoid looking where I don't want to travel. If I look at a tree, that may lead to being 'as one' with it—something I would rather not be! When I emerge from a tree run, I relish having dashed among the trees rather than into them. See the snow, not the tree, is my mantra for tree runs.

Take the plunge

On steeps I "take the plunge" with each turn. Doing so adds thrill and is very effective in ensuring that my skis turn (and that I remain upright!). I finish each turn with my skis mostly across the slope then let gravity and momentum draw my upper body down through space towards the start of the next turn. Taking the plunge, with gravity and momentum pulling my upper body and my viewpoint down towards the valley floor—*gasp!*—begs to have my skis turn so they can catch me and slow my descent. **The key to having my skis turn easily is to ensure that between turns the tip-to-tail slope of my skis matches the slope of the hill.** By letting my upper body be taken by gravity and momentum while my feet cross under me, I move through an orientation at mid transition where my body is perpendicular to the slope so my skis match the slope. As my switch proceeds my skis get tilted and positioned to grip the snow and catch me—halting my 'perilous' plunge. At least until the next plunge and repeat...

On steeps, between turns I want to move through an early-in-the-turn orientation in which the tip-to-tail slope of my skis matches the slope of the hill. This allows my skis to start their turn in response to the turning of my legs and feet, and then to 'catch' me while they complete their turn.

6 Recap and Review

Sometimes saying something a little differently adds insight and helps the learning process. This section revisits selected topics to help you to better understand and synthesize points that are yet to connect. It can also serve as a quick reference and refresher for you from time to time.

Exit each turn with momentum

Exit the turn with skis and upper body on their own trajectories— and on target to where you plan them to be when forces build in the next turn. The trajectory of your skis will be influenced by the tilt and aim that you apply to them during the transition (by turning legs and feet). The trajectory of your upper body will be along its line of momentum to the inside of where your skis will travel. When the lines of travel of your skis and upper body converge, and your preparation for the turn matches exactly with your prediction of how it will feel and what the result will be, you will have experienced beauty in motion.

The X-Factor

While both need to occur during the transition, crossunder trumps crossover. Concentrate on having your feet move across under your upper body (crossunder), rather than on getting your upper body to move across your feet (crossover). **Persist your edging effort long enough so your skis take your feet across under you while momentum floats your upper body (and viewpoint) towards the next turn.** Use your momentum and edging skills so the tilt of your body at the exit of one turn compared to its reoriented tilt at the start of the next turn creates an "X".

Use the Hump

Feeling and exploiting the virtual hump is one of the joys of skiing. To feel the virtual hump you will need some speed—don't look for its effect in slow zones. Generally you will experience the hump anytime your skis arc as you flow out of a turn and your body gets reoriented from one turn to the next within a relatively short time. As your feet move from beside to under you, your body will be pushed upwards to the extent that you don't shorten your posture to compensate for the apparent rise in the snow.[30] You can even get airborne with a well timed extension, a jump at the hump. Have fun with it!

Be patient early

Each turn has a 'patience zone' in which I weigh a little less than normal and can relax a bit while preparing for the forces of the upcoming turn. This zone is in the latter part of the transition where my skis begin to find their line before turning forces escalate. I use this brief time to fine-tune my balance, since I'm light and can adjust my posture without working against heavy forces. **Good use of the 'patience zone' sets me up for a smooth and balanced entry to the turn**, and, keeps me from rushing my moves. Interestingly, I can be patient and fast at the same time...

Float like a butterfly, sting like a bee

Balancing atop big changes in underfoot pressure is one of the pleasures of skiing. I edge my skis then balance on the forces that arise, seeking a smooth increase in pressure with each turn, followed by a much reduced (and at times a near absence of) pressure during the ensuing transition. **Fine-tuning my balance and posture in the patience zone allows me to handle more force in the turn**, which adds to the fun. It's a 'pressure' skiing this way...

Face your momentum

Upper body—the pelvis, chest, shoulders, arms and hands—should all face the direction that momentum would take you in if your skis suddenly had no grip. The torso and arms being square to momentum provides a good directional reference between turns and the most robust angle for dealing with nuances in upcoming terrain. Note that turning the head freely as needed works well: doing so doesn't disturb balance or flow since it changes very little the distribution of body mass, *but doing so is important for looking where you are going!*

---

[30] To simulate the mechanics involved, stand a pen on a desktop and tilt it from side to side. Each time it moves from tilted to vertical the top end of the pen gets pushed away from the desk surface—the identical effect happens as your body goes from tilted in the turn to vertical in the transition. In effect, while skiing you need to shorten the pen.

My chest, torso and arms face my line of momentum, but my head turn reveals that my eyes are seeking something different—where I want to travel! (Note the direction of head versus torso in the above image).

Dexterity down under

Thighs are the engines of turn, fine-tuning the tilt and aim of the skis relative to the baseline tilt and aim as driven by the skier's posture and balance centerpoint. ***A skilled skier will be able to move their legs independently of any involvement or influence by their upper body.*** Concentrating all balance related movements in the legs merges the acts of balancing with controlling where the skis will travel. Developing leg-turning dexterity is well worth the time and effort.[31]

---

[31] I've seen guidance to move, tilt or rotate the upper body as a means to adjust the skis. I avoid all of these (other than in exceptional recovery situations) in order to avoid complicating my efforts to balance.

During the turn

In the turn, I resist and balance atop the forces that arise up through my feet. I let **the forces of the turn compress my body into a dynamic-looking position by mid-to-late in the turn** (legs turned, knees bent, body hinged at hip joint, upper body facing momentum). The weight I feel is my friend, pressuring my skis so they grip reliably and give me a solid 'ledge' to balance on.

Gentle turns

Not every turn is a laid-over screamer on groomed runs. Gentler turns go as such. Stand with your skis across the hill and push with your poles. Flatten your skis so they begin to change direction down the hill, seemingly automatically. Turn your legs (but not your torso) to 'go with' your skis as they begin changing direction, then balance and ride while your skis make their turn—**concentrate on balancing, not turning, and let your skis alone deliver the change in direction as you balance on them**. You should end up balancing mostly on your outside ski as it moves across to under you while the turn develops. All the while, keep the pressure of your boot cuffs on your shins and calves as equal and as steady as possible. Figure 35 shows flattening the skis by letting the whole body become perpendicular to the hill to get the turn started.

TIP   When skiing, move 'through' rather 'to' any given posture, position or image that you equate with skiing. Seek to move continuously, remain athletic and agile, and avoid freezing in any given posture or position.

O'er that magic carpet!

Imagining that you are standing on a small carpet can produce *'magic'*—or at least make it easier to balance, especially in powder and moguls. **Keep your feet within a small area and tidily 'under' you to create a stable and strong platform.** This approach works wonders in virtually any situation and is especially helpful in dealing with large changes in pressure and friction often encountered in soft snow and moguls. Figure 35 shows keeping the feet on the magic carpet.

Ride the _small_ 'magic carpet'

Body perpendicular to the slope flattens skis and they begin to turn

Turn legs to edge and aim skis as they turn

Hold thighs turned and ride the skis around the turn

Figure 35. Imagine a small carpet that is just large enough to encircle your bindings when your feet are a boot width or so apart. When skiing, keep both feet on the carpet at all times—don't let them wander beyond the edges of the carpet. You should feel very balanced, directly over your feet. Magic!

Simplify your balancing act

To simplify balancing, minimize the number of variables you need to deal with. ***Keep your body movements to a minimum as you tilt and aim your skis, then balance using balance feedback cues such as how your boots feel.*** Tilt and aim your skis using only your legs—think: below the hip sockets, or, outside the buns (ha!). Keep your upper body quiet and cooperative—positioned and ready to make recovery moves when the going gets wild. Adding effort to tilt or rotate your upper body relative to your legs only adds unnecessary complexity that you will need to counter in some way. As is often true, simpler is better...

Turning under pressure

Underfoot pressure accompanies any change in our line of travel. The weight we feel, other than due to gravity alone, changes with any change in direction to our line of travel, left, right, up or down. Pressure on our skis that deflects our mass is usually described in the context of turns (sideways forces) but can be just as relevant to rises in the snow, even virtual humps (vertical forces). To make well-executed turns, we flex laterally in order to edge our skis and balance laterally, and flex vertically (mostly using hip and knee joints) to preserve our balance while the snow rises and falls under us.

Let 'em turn you

Think 'balance', rather than think 'turn'. When you tilt your skis and balance on them, they turn you. Move your legs in order to tilt (rather than turn) your skis, and then balance and ride while they turn.[32]

Fix the snowplow hangover

I often see early stage skiers exhibiting a 'snowplow hangover'—they lock their outside leg straight and push their outside (downhill) ski sideways, bracing against gravity. These people are fighting gravity rather than enjoying the momentum it creates.[33] A first change to better and easier skiing is to **let their upper body tilt forward over their outside knee.** This has the dual effect of bending at the knees and balancing mostly on the outside ski. Bent knees allow them to control the tilt of their skis by turning their legs, not possible with a straight outside leg braced and reached out to the side. The final step is to feel centered in their boots while turning their legs and balancing throughout the ride of the turn. Figure 36 illustrates the prescribed changes.

---

[32] Pictures of skiers at mid turn encourage learners of the sport to seek a legs-out-to-the-side skis-on-edge position. Trying to then turn rather than balance leads to twisting the upper body towards the inside of the turn, outside hand across in front of the chest, and the skis still refusing to turn—and sooner or later an awkward twisting fall (maybe only one…)

[33] They may be victims of having successfully developed a reliance on the 'snowplow' position to control speed, and an engrained response to fear being to stick a leg out straight to slow, turn, or stop.

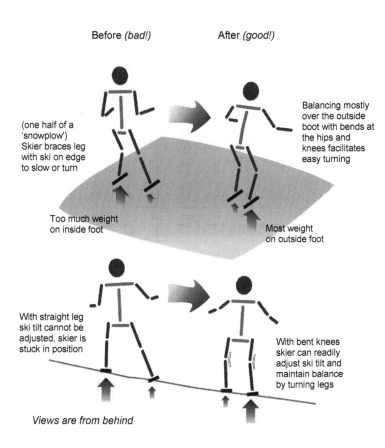

Before *(bad!)*   After *(good!)*

Balancing mostly over the outside boot with bends at the hips and knees facilitates easy turning

(one half of a 'snowplow') Skier braces leg with ski on edge to slow or turn

Too much weight on inside foot

Most weight on outside foot

With straight leg ski tilt cannot be adjusted, skier is stuck in position

With bent knees skier can readily adjust ski tilt and maintain balance by turning legs

Views are from behind

Figure 36. Fixing the snowplow hangover. Balancing over the outside foot and turning legs to control ski tilt is a move towards shedding the habit of bracing against gravity that may have roots in relying on a 'snowplow' to stop or turn.

Feel groovy

Edge your skis and balance while they carry you through a turn, and **leave clean grooves in the snow as evidence of a steady ride**. Better to be 'feeling groovy' (on skis that are tilted and producing a reliable grip) than to be 'slip sliding away' (out of control on skis with too little tilt and grip).

The sole knows

With equal pressure on your shin and calf, what you feel on your sole reflects the pressure on your ski. Feeling your weight distributed along the arch side of your outside foot means your weight is distributed along the inside edge of your outside ski. As long as your weight is centered in the fore and aft direction (equal weight on forefoot and heel, and equal pressure on shin and calf) your ski is optimally pressured to perform a turn. When balanced in a turn the pressure distribution on the soles of your feet should approximate Figure 37.

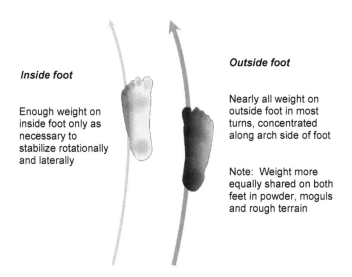

Inside foot

Enough weight on inside foot only as necessary to stabilize rotationally and laterally

Outside foot

Nearly all weight on outside foot in most turns, concentrated along arch side of foot

Note: Weight more equally shared on both feet in powder, moguls and rough terrain

Figure 37. Pressure on the feet during a turn, as the sole feels it. Darker means more pressure.

How I Ski

Diff'rent strokes

I'd rather edge and glide than pivot and slide, though both have their place depending on terrain and snow conditions. Edging and gliding on cleanly arcing skis invokes speed—fun but not universally applicable in all terrain situations and snow conditions. Having my skis skid a little as they carve their turns (skidded carves) allows me to throttle my speed and gives me lots of options for dealing with tricky terrain. I can ski a wide range of speeds and paths depending on the amount of ski tilt and skid I incorporate in a given turn. Pivoting and sliding allows me to set up for a direction change while slowing myself—I add tilt after pivoting to add grip and deflect my line of travel, contain my pace in demanding terrain, or to stop. ***Regardless of the type of turn, my game plan is to turn my legs as the leading move to tilt and aim my skis, and then balance on my skis while they perform the turn.***

Adaptability – the summit

When does the quest for better technique end? When is enough enough? The good news is probably never, since there's always room for improvement, and the satisfaction of achievement that accompanies improvement is always rewarding. My journey is about accumulating and honing skills so I can ski with expertise whatever terrain and snow conditions I encounter. This means taking opportunities as they arise (provided they are safe) to test myself—challenge my ability to stay balanced and upright—even if it isn't video-worthy. Remember, if you are standing on a pair skis while they carry you down a hill, you are skiing. And ***if you are still standing after skiing something that previously you wouldn't, you are skiing better.***[34]

---

[34] Whistler Blackcomb is famous for its myriad terrain choices, its wide range of snow conditions, and its abundance of the 'white' stuff. If you can ski with confidence at Whistler, you will be well prepared to ski any resort on the planet. Highly recommended for the skier who seeks the full gamut within one ski area.

7   Foibles and Fixes

Through my own learning and while teaching others I've seen several typical foibles that arise repeatedly. Often a simple focus can provide a fix. Here are a few of my favorites, with a likely cause and a recommended remedy.

"My skis want to travel straight instead of turn, and I end up falling to the inside."

Likely cause: you are entering the turn standing on your heels, so the tails of your skis cut in and run straight, leading you to lean inside as a means to 'will' your skis to turn. When you fall inside, this reduces the weight on your skis and they run even straighter, worsening the situation.

Remedy: pull both feet back to establish your centerpoint under the arch of your outside boot before the turn begins. Seek equal pressure on your shin and calf, with weight distributed along the arch side of your outside boot. Strive to feel weight along the whole length of your foot as your ski starts its turn and keep that feeling as your ski rides you through the turn.

"My outside ski travels straight while my inside ski turns, and I end up resembling a hood ornament (after a full layout face plant)."

Likely cause: you have too much weight on your inside foot, and, likely, whatever weight you have on your outside foot is on its heel. With this setup, your inside ski often points to the inside of the turn (skis are splayed, their tips wider apart than their tails). In the worst situation, you have your knees slightly pinched together (1970's skier syndrome) which causes the edge of your inside ski to catch on the snow.

Remedy: keep your feet on the 'magic carpet', hold them under you and aim them parallel to each other. Balance over the middle of your outside boot *before* the turn begins, and keep the weight distribution on the sole of your outside foot steady while the turn progresses. Turn legs and feet in unison to help keep your skis parallel.

"My skis seem to have a mind of their own, going too fast and not always in the same direction."

Likely cause: your boots may fit poorly, with a sloppy or loose feeling and possibly an air gap between your boot cuff and your shin and calf. Any looseness around the feet in combination with excessive 'give' by the inner boot compromises how well any control you attempt with your legs and feet actually affect the tilt and aim of your skis.

Remedy: seek a good boot fitter to reduce the looseness, and consider updating your boots in the process. Get a well-fitting foot bed too.

"I feel forever stuck in the back seat, my calves hammering against the backs of my boots, especially during turns". Or,

"My legs burn after only a few turns, and I look forward to the end of the day way earlier than I'd like to."

Likely cause: you are standing mostly on your heels, and when your skis grip in a turn they move ahead of your upper body and you end up in the 'armchair position', using a lot of thigh muscle to keep your backside out of the snow.

Remedy: seek to be centered fore and aft at all times, feeling weight along the whole of your soles, that is, with toe, ball, arch and heel all sharing the load, and equal pressure on your shins and calves. Try skiing slowly while experimenting with more weight on the balls of your feet; press down a little as if beginning to 'stand on your toes'. Once you feel steady on the 'whole foot' at slow speeds, try for the same feeling at faster speeds. Feel toe, ball, arch and heel all engaged.

"My skis always slip sideways during a turn—I can't get them to leave clean grooves in the snow."

Likely causes (some or all of the following): insufficient tilt on the skis, pressing shins forward into boot cuffs during a turn (which encourages ski tails to skid), focusing on making the skis change direction rather than letting them change direction based on their tilt and pressure, fear of speed and a safety reflex to pivot the skis so they skid and brake, unable to edge the skis without pivoting them (no turning of legs, or, turning the legs is tightly linked to turning the feet and pivoting the skis).

Remedy: find a smooth slope that isn't very steep and let your skis run lengthwise, tails tracking tips, while you tilt them then simply balance while they turn. Just turn your thighs, then balance, maintaining a forward bend at the hip joints. As the turn progresses, advance your outside foot in order to keep your weight centered over its arch and boot cuff pressure equal on the shin and calf of your outside leg.

"When I let my skis arc a couple of turns I end up traveling way too fast. I didn't like the scare that gave me!"

Likely cause: the snow is too firm or too steep (or a bit of both) for skiing at a manageable speed using pure arc turns.

Remedy: use skidded turns so your skis slip sideways gradually while they carve their path—this will create friction and contain your speed. Be sure your skis 'finish' their turns, and travel quite *across* the slope during your switch. Find a wide open gentle groomed slope where your speed won't build too much and experiment with how your skis react to different amounts of tilt.

"As the snow gets skied out on a powdery day I keep getting caught way in the back seat."

Likely cause: as the snow gets skied out, it gets shallower and firmer and thus provides less friction to help keep your speed in check. Your feet can easily move ahead of your upper body if you anticipate friction and slowing of your skis which do not occur.

Remedy: establish good fore and aft balance going into each turn, studying the upcoming snow for how much resistance your skis are likely to encounter. Keep bent forward at the hip joints, with your core muscles engaged—as if to resist someone pulling your upper body ahead, or pulling your feet ahead and out from under you—so that you can deal with greater or lesser slowing than you anticipate.

"My skis chatter through every turn—and my teeth are rattling!"

Likely cause: your skis are slipping sideways during each carve just enough to invoke the chatter. The problem is typical on harder snow when skiing too slowly for the skis to grip and arc their turn cleanly, and is common with skis that have poor dampening characteristics.

Remedy: find ways to concentrate more pressure on the ski during their change in direction. Try skiing faster, tilting the skis more, or shortening the distance over which the turn occurs (any of these will increase the pressure on the skis while they turn). The alternative is to flatten the skis and let them skid more during each turn (this is the conservative approach, especially if you can't get your skis to grip the snow reliably).

"I can't get a steady view, things are always bouncing around."

Likely cause: too tense overall, holding muscles tightly to compensate for a hard-to-maintain posture. You may also notice an imbalance of pressure from your boot cuffs on your shins and calves.

Remedy: Relax; especially the shoulders and upper back. Tilt forward a little at the hip joints, and peer through the upper half of your goggles. Hold hands where you can see them, hold poles as loosely as possible. Think: ready, centered, and relaxed. Relax ankles, turn legs, balance.

"I avoid steep slopes because I can't get my skis to turn—I then go too fast, and end up crashing big time."

Likely cause: leaning into the hill. This is a natural reaction to feeling exposed, since it keeps your body close to the hill (for better stability) and your skis between you and the valley (for a safer feeling). Unfortunately, leaning into the hill usually causes your skis to slip sideways, which negates their ability to 'finish' their turn and then carry your feet across the slope to switch you into the next turn.

Remedy: allow your internal barbell to move through perpendicular to the slope between turns. Late in the turn, balance mainly on your outside ski with it edged strongly into the snow, then let momentum take your feet across the slope while gravity and momentum pull your upper body across over your feet. All that's left is to point your knees down the slope; your skis will turn and ultimately 'catch' your mass as they round out their turn.

"In moguls I keep getting stuck traversing, looking for a good place to turn."

Likely cause: poor balance at the end of the turn. This results in just enough hesitation that you break the flow into your switch and subsequent turn, and the result is 'shopping' for the next place to turn.

Remedy: keep your feet feeling directly under you, on the 'magic carpet', especially late in the turn when forces are greatest (and magnified when the turn ends on a bump). With your feet right under you, it is easier to have your skis direct your feet across under you to drive your switch. Your switch occurring immediately out of turn will help you maintain a continuous flow into the next turn, and the next and the next...

"My ski tips keep crossing when I turn, usually my outside tip under my inside tip. It's really annoying."

Likely cause: Outside ski is tilted (or edged) more than the inside ski, or, the outside leg is turned more than needed. In either case, the outside ski turns sharper than the inside ski, cutting under as the turn begins.

Remedy: Turn the outside leg a little less, or possibly, turn the inside leg and foot more to encourage the inside ski to stay parallel to the outside ski. Imagine holding a volleyball between your knees to ensure the inside knee points well inside the turn. Be sure to turn both legs an equal amount and at the same time.

"My skis skid out at the end of the turn, and I have a hard time getting into the next turn."

Likely cause: Weight is progressing forward (or staying forward) late in the turn; you may feel your shins mashing into your boot cuffs. Forward directed pressure on the boots releases pressure from the tails of the skis and they then slip sideways. Or, because the skis aren't turning by themselves, the reaction is to twist the chest and shoulders into the turn, which flattens the skis on the snow; they lose edge grip and offer nothing underfoot from which to move into the next turn.

Remedy: Balance where the pressure on your shins and calves are equal going into the turn, then advance your outside foot so you continue to feel equal pressure on your shins and calves throughout the turn. That will improve edge grip late in the turn, making it easy to start your switch.

"My skis wash out sideways going into every turn. I keep 'spinning out' like a Formula One driver having a bad day."

Likely cause: Upper body is rotating in the direction of the anticipated turn, before the skis have the turn established. This reduces ski tilt as well as induces pivoting to the skis, and they slip sideways as a result.

Remedy: Turn the legs to lead the skis through the transition, without turning your upper body—just let it be, facing straight ahead. Be patient and let the skis start turning under you and concentrate on balance as your feet and skis become turned across the pelvis. Ease your weight onto the outside foot and then ease the foot forward to keep balanced over it throughout the turn. Turn legs, balance and ride.

8   Ski Prepared

Get today's skis and boots

'Pencils' and rear-entry boots—the equipment of decades past—are extinct and thankfully gone the way of the dodo bird. Pencils lacked the torsional stiffness to grip the snow and carve turns as readily as today's skis. Turning pencils required a move that is equally extinct as the equipment: a forward lunge against the tongues of our boots to pressure the ski tips so they would grip the snow and trigger a sudden swivel into a new direction. New skis grip the snow very effectively given better materials and construction as well as (generally) a deeper sidecut. All that's needed is some tilt on the snow and pressure through their waists and they will readily perform turns for us. One thing hasn't changed: boots are still as important as ever for edging and holding the skis tilted on the snow. Be sure to find a competent boot fitter who can select a boot according to the type of foot you have and supply you with a custom or equally effective pair of foot beds. You'll want a boot shell that matches your ankle and foot type, foot beds that align your knees properly over your feet so your feet are comfortable and stable while under load, and boot cuffs adjusted so your skis remain flat when you move your shins forward and back. Aim for a stiffer rather than a softer shell to give you more control. Generally, stiffer boots allow more demanding and precise skiing, softer boots suit easier riding with less precise edge control.

Keep fit and flexible

Skiing requires suitable movements and postures, even when challenging and unsettling sensations arise from underfoot. Fitness and flexibility help deal with foibles that may occur when venturing anew and learning new skills. Fitness adds strength for moving through positions amidst forces that are unfamiliar to everyday living. Flexibility reduces the chance of injury during a vigorous effort to recover balance or an awkward tumble. I recommend keeping fit through regular exercise, or at a minimum embark on a multi-week preparation leading up to a ski trip, to strengthen the core and legs, and enhance flexibility of the legs and back.

Practice and visualize whenever you wish you were skiing

Mastery of anything requires knowledge, practice and repetition. The good news is that skills can be attained at any age, as long as a person wants to learn and improve, believes they are able to, and works at it. Skiing is highly technique-centric—that is, correctly applied skiing-specific knowledge makes a huge difference in how easy and fun the sport can be. In my experience with skiing—as with golf, another sport where technique is a huge swing factor[35]—my proficiency advanced dramatically when I learned effective methods and then practiced them over and over until they became automatic and natural. Since ski areas can be distant and time intervals between ski trips can be more than a memory horizon, it helps to do something when not on skis that will help you once you are. I recommend practicing the "*Key Postures and Movements*" and visualizing—replaying in your mind skiing in various situations, 'seeing' and 'feeling' how you want it to be. Even if your internalized technique is suboptimal, visualization will establish a baseline reference from which to pursue improvements the next time you are skiing.

---

[35] That's my last pun!

9 Closing Thoughts

Skiing is a sport of millimeters

Any time my weight acts through my skis at other than my fore aft centerpoint, I am less than perfectly balanced. Just as baseball can be a "sport of inches", where the ball flies hundreds of feet but outs are determined within inches, in skiing, the distances are also large, but whether I'm "out" balance-wise can be gauged in millimeters. Any misalignment by even a few millimeters of my center of mass, my centerpoint, and the collective forces acting up through my feet can mean the difference between balancing perfectly and falling slowly.

Flow requires tails tracking tips

If we balance on tilted skis they slide with tails tracking tips, and we experience a smooth ride as our skis slide lengthwise along the snow. If the snow is rippled, our skis sliding lengthwise will deliver a smoother and more predictable ride than if they were to slide sideways across the same ripples. To picture the difference, consider skis sliding down a flight of stairs in a lengthwise manner, bridging the gaps between steps and smoothing out the ride, versus pounding sideways from step to step. Always aim your skis to slide tails tracking tips in order to achieve and enjoy a smooth flow.

Balance so your skis turn you

In every turn, I seek to feel balanced exactly over my centerpoint, with pressure along the arch side of my outside boot to hold my ski firmly on a given tilt. When I feel my weight centered as such, my skis make their own turns and I can readily maintain my balance even when large changes in weight occur, especially in bumpy terrain. The optimum centerpoint may vary a little from person to person—experiment to find where you feel your weight centered on your feet when your skis are making turns easily and naturally, and where you remain in balance while they do so. Ultimately, you should find that your skis progress smoothly through each turn while your upper body rides relaxed (other than to resist the increased weight of the turn) without needing to correct for imbalances.

Expert knowledge and instruction—priceless!!

In the pursuit of expert skiing, nothing tops expert in-person guidance and feedback. A keen and experienced eye and the harsh reality of video playback can often reveal issues that may otherwise go unnoticed—masked by old compensating habits that offer confidence through familiarity, even though they compromise your skiing potential. Seek a coach or instructor who can communicate objectives clearly, pinpoint an aspect that needs work, and guide you through a drill or exercise that will lead you to new awareness and skills. Greater knowledge, skills, and enjoyment await us all, given the right mentor.

> *"Skiing is all about*
>
> *how, when and where you stand*
>
> *...and who you're with"*

Terminology

Body: the whole body, legs, torso, head and arms. Body parts are connected to each other by joints.

Torso / Trunk: pelvis, spine and shoulders plus associated muscles, including the buttocks.

Upper Body: torso, head and arms.

Lower Body: everything from the thighs (or femurs) down through the toes—thighs, knees, shins, calves, ankles and feet.

Legs: femurs, knees, tibias and fibulas; thighs and calves. Hip joints, ankles and feet are not part of the legs.

Ankles, Knees, Hips: primary joints of the lower body used for controlling the tilt and aim of the skis. Hips means ball joints or hip sockets.

Posture: relative position of body parts while standing.

Dynamic: changing posture in an athletic or active manner.

Bending: moving to reduce or shrink the angle between two adjoining body parts. Bending major joints reduces body height.

Extending: opposite of bending: moving at one or more joints so the adjoining body parts straighten with respect to each other. If I extend my body, I get taller; if I extend my leg, my knee straightens.

Flexing: refers to both bending and extending.

Absolute Vertical: parallel to the force of gravity, as a plumb bob hangs.

Vertical: the direction in which I sense my weight is acting. In my ready position, vertical is parallel to a line from my head to my feet.

Mass: the collective mass of my body, skis, boots, clothing, helmet, and poles.

Momentum: in physics, mass multiplied by velocity, where velocity is speed in a given direction. When skiing, momentum acts to force my mass to continue traveling along my line of momentum.

Weight: force acting downwards through my feet that feels like my weight at a given instant. Vector sum of static weight (as on a bathroom scale), plus forces related to deflection and pulse.

Centerpoint: the center of where our weight is distributed on the soles of our feet. We can hold the most weight on our preferred centerpoint.

Lateral: sideways to the direction that my torso faces or the direction in which I'm traveling. Lateral forces on my skis deflect me sideways to my line of momentum, and cause me to be carried along a curved path.

Rotate: movement or effort acting around an axis, i.e., I can choose to rotate my upper body around its vertical axis, but I try not to do so.

Tilt: orientation relative to a reference, such as the body's vertical axis, or the slope of the hill.

Edging: moving in order to adjust or control the tilt of the skis relative to what I sense as vertical.

Direction: the direction of travel at a given instant in time, generally, in a lateral rather than vertical sense.

Deflection: the distance travelled laterally during a turn. Deflection is the result of turning forces that I feel up through my feet while my skis change my line of travel.

Pulse: a brief thrust of pressure applied downward through feet and skis. I create a pulse by either extending my legs suddenly, or tensing my legs to halt my body dropping (as when landing after a jump or compressing into a turn in powder snow). A pulse can increase deflection within a given distance.

Turn: the curved path of travel that my skis carry me along according to their tilt, pressure, and lengthwise bend.

Transition: the distance or elapsed time from where one turn ends and the next one starts.

Switch: the lateral transposition of my feet and torso between turns, my feet crossing under my torso while my torso crosses over my feet.

Pivot: (as in pivot of the skis) forcing my skis to point in a different direction than they naturally choose based on their tilt, pressure and bend, by applying a rotational force through my boots.

Apex (of a turn): the point in a turn where deflection forces are strongest, my weight is heaviest, and my direction change is quickest.

Arc: a turn in which the tail of a ski slides through the identical line that was traced by its tip. Arcing results in turns of maximum efficiency and speed.

Carve: akin to arc, in that my skis perform a turn shape in response to their tilt, pressure and bend.

Skid: when my skis point partially or fully sideways to the line that they are sliding along. Skidding creates friction and slows the speed of my feet. I can use skidding to adjust my balance, reduce speed, or slide to a stop.

Acknowledgments

Much of my recent learning regarding ski technique can be particularly attributed to two gentlemen who are highly talented in their respective specialties. I thank them for sharing their understanding and helping me to learn the related skills. Both are long time Whistler skiers.

Mark Anderson — Ski racing coach, former member of Canadian National Alpine Ski Team

Ken Paynter — Ski racing coach and performance skiing instructor, Canadian Ski Instructors Alliance Level 4

Thank you to my many friends and reviewers who offered constructive feedback on the content of the book, which after discussion, reflection and rework, led to improvements for the benefit of all future readers.

Also a warm thanks to Stuart Stephen, an avid mountain guide and photographer who contributed many of the photos.

Finally a special thanks to Maureen, my 'better half', for her unwavering support, patient reading, and helpful feedback since the earliest days of the book's first edition.

Thank you for your interest in this book. I invite your feedback and any general or specific interest you may have regarding its content. My contact info is at www.skiwellsimply.com.

Best wishes,

Ken Chaddock